In **The Help, Hope, and Cope Book for People With Aging Parents,** Patricia Rushford offers insight and encouragement for helping elderly parents who are experiencing the detrimental effects of aging. By using this reliable guide, you can be sure that you're providing the best care possible. The author draws upon her professional experience as she discusses concerns that are on your heart. The extensive list of subjects covered includes:

- *developing good relationships with elderly parents*
- *facing death with hope and peace*
- *prolonging your parents' independence*
- *healing negative and hurtful feelings*
- *celebrating life and making it more enjoyable*

BY   Patricia H. Rushford

Have You Hugged Your Teenager Today?
The Care & Feeding of Sick Kids
From Money Mess to Money Management
The Help, Hope, and Cope Book for People With
    Aging Parents

PATRICIA H. RUSHFORD

The Help, Hope and Cope Book
for People with Aging Parents

Fleming H. Revell Company
Old Tappan, New Jersey

Library of Congress Cataloging in Publication Data

Rushford, Patricia H.
   The help, hope, and cope book for people with aging parents.

   Bibliography: p.
   1. Parents, Aged—United States—Care and hygiene.
   2. Parents, Aged—United States—Family relationships.
   3. Adult children—United States.   I. Title.
   HQ1063.6.R87   1985   646.7′8   84-27631
   ISBN 0-8007-1248-X

This book is dedicated to those who instilled in me a heart full of love and compassion for the elderly:

Those who have died,

> Hjalmer Anderson, my dad
> Dagfin and Petra Olsen, my grandparents
> Grandad and Cora Stephens

Those who live on,

> Dagny Anderson, my mom
> Uncle Gunder Olsen
> Aunt Olga Bond

And to the others in my very special family who are growing older, but better, every day.

Contents

Acknowledgments   10
Introduction   11

1 Suddenly They're Older   13

What Can We Do?—Semi-Independent and Loving
It—How Old Is an Aging Parent?—The Generational
Sandwich—So Where Do We Start?

2 Aging's Just Another Word for Growing Up   18

Aging Awareness Test—The Myths and Realities of
Aging—A Long and Happy Senility to All?—You
Can't Teach an Old Dog New Tricks–Or Can You?—
Slowing Down Doesn't Mean STOP—". . . The Dust
Returns to the Earth . . ."—Turning It Off Versus
Getting It On—Is Sex for Seniors?—The Poverty of
Age

3 Emotions   28

How Does It Feel to Grow Old?—Sometimes I'm
Afraid—The Grief of Old Age—Feelings—The Emo-
tional Side of Aging—Mixed Up? Congratulations—
You're Normal—"Be Angry, But Do Not Sin . . ."
—". . . What I Don't Want to Do I Do . . ."—"I

Feel Guilty (Resentful, Angry) Because . . . "—Finding Solutions—"I've Got to Talk to Somebody"

4 Guilt 40

A Guilt by Any Other Name—Freedom From Guilt Is Easy When It's Real—"Fix Your Thoughts on What Is True and Good . . ."—"A Merry Heart Doeth Good . . ."—"Beloved, Let Us Love One Another . . ."

5 When the Time Comes 47

"What Are We Going to Do?"—Evaluate: Do They Really Need Your Help?—Should You Intervene?—Talk It Over—List Your Alternatives—Taking Action

6 Where Will They Live? 57

From Baby Boom to Aging Boom—Living Alone and Loving It—The Migratory "Snowbirds"—Staying Home—Having Your Home and Selling It Too—Mobile Homes—Retirement Havens—Shared Housing—Semi-Independent Living Harder to Find—Sheltered Housing—Foster Homes—Bringing Parents Into Your Home—Nursing Homes

7 Maintaining Independence: How You Can Help 67

"A Place of My Own"—Little Things Mean a Lot—Put Yourself in a Wheelchair—Through the Looking Glass Dimly—Hearing Loss—Speech Impairment—Loss of Taste, Smell, Touch . . .—"Am I Losing My Mind?"—Afraid to Leave Your Parent Alone?—A Need to Be Needed—Social Contacts—God Never Said, "Go Retire"

8 Alzheimer's: The Disease of the Century 80

What It Is—Identifying Alzheimer's—The Four Phases—What Alzheimer's Is Not—Who Get's Alz-

heimer's Disease?—Is Alzheimer's Treatable?—Help
for the Hopeless

9 Common Illnesses and Symptoms Affecting the Elderly   90

Arthritis—Bronchitis and Other Lung Problems—
Cancer—Diabetes—Heart Disease—Hypertension—
Stroke—Other Common Complaints and Symptoms

10 Home Care   108

Pace Yourself—Learn to Meet Their Needs—The
Nursing Care Plan—Physical Needs—Cleanliness:
Good Hygiene and Grooming—Exercise Needs—
Feed Them Right—Social and Psychological Needs—
Reality Orientation—No One Ever Said It Would Be
Easy

11 Nursing Home Care—Your Role   125

When Do You Consider Nursing Home Care?—What
Is a Nursing Home?—Choosing a Nursing Home—
When the Choice Is Made—The Contract—Cancel-
ing Guilt—Making the Move—How You Can Help—
What Do You Say After You've Said, "Hello"?—The
Comfort and Care Clause—Other Personal Needs—
Clothing Needs and Care—Meeting Mental and
Emotional Needs—You Can Make a Difference

12 Finances and Legalities   141

Insurance—Medicare—Medicaid—Lawyers and Legalities—Wills—Power of Attorney—Joint Ownership—Trusts—Guardianship—What   About   a
Stubborn Parent?—When Do You Step In?—Is There
Gold in Them Thar Years?—Supplemental Income
for the Elderly—Investments in the "Golden
Years"—Funeral Arrangements

13 Aging: The Final Frontier 159

Facing the Inevitable—Understanding Death—What Do You Say to a Dying Man?—Talk About It—Helping Gram Die—Learn From the Children—Comes the Sorrow—"Two of a Kind"

14 More Help and Where to Find It 170

Additional Reading (Comprehensive Bibliography)—Addresses of Volunteer and Government Agencies—Patient's Bill of Rights—How to Choose a Nursing Home Checklist

Acknowledgments

My special thanks to:

Ron, my husband, who continues to love me.

Ruby MacDonald and Lauraine Snelling for their uplifting praise and critique.

Pastors Dan Dowling, Dale Gunderson, and Larry Jahnke for their inspirational and expert critique and help.

Judy Allman, R.N., B.S.N.; Kathy James, L.P.N.; Angela Johnson, freelance writer; Shirley Lawson, R.N., B.S.N.; Margo Power, R.N. and freelance writer; Elaine Teutsch, R.N., M.N.; Allan Alexander, M.D.; Patty Newton, M.D.; George Telisman, Director of the SW Washington Agency on Aging; David Walker, Deputy Commissioner, Senior Citizen Program State of Washington; and the people at Staff Builders Health Care Services, for their professional advice and critique.

Christine McLachlan of Omega Printing whose encouragement and praise never ceases.

Ken Mathys of The Sound Alternatives, for his critique and constant support.

My kids, David and Caryl, who I hope will read this when they need *Help, Hope, and Cope* with their *Aging Parents.*

And to those very special people, the aging, whose wisdom and experience makes them our nation's most valuable resource.

Introduction

Age is not all decay: it is the ripening, the swelling, of the fresh life within, that withers and bursts the husks.

GEORGE MACDONALD
The Marquis of Lossie

The other day a patient suffering from "rumitzm" grumbled, "Don't bother helping me, Doc. We're all growing older; it just gets me down."

Yes, age relentlessly advances on everyone. But you need not take this helpless, hopeless, and copeless attitude—especially when these children of Father Time are your own parents.

Do you want to help your aging parents? Does the job seem so complex that you hardly know where to start? Patricia Rushford supplies the information (help), prescribes the attitudes (hope), and outlines the skills (cope) that you need to tackle the challenge.

Mid-life brims with challenging dilemmas—mortgage payments, rebellious teenagers, and aging parents. At some point, most middle-aged adults must ask themselves the difficult question: "How can I enhance my parents' happiness and comfort while still encouraging them to maintain their own individuality and integrity?"

Successful coping with any big problem requires preparation. When you have prepared to handle your problems, then you can see them as challenging opportunities. In fact, problems provide the God-given method for growth in maturity—the bigger the problem, the greater the possibilities. After properly equipping yourself with the necessary information, attitudes, and skills—you will be able to learn and grow in helping your parents. It is here that this book comes in.

Up-to-date and informative, *The Help, Hope, and Cope Book* . . . is a complete guide to dealing with your aging parents. This is not a textbook by some ivory tower scholar who tries to baffle you with all the latest research on the aging process. Rather, this is an extremely practical book by a woman who has made practical caring for suffering people her life's business.

11

Realizing that each situation is unique, Patricia Rushford outlines strategies for handling many difficult situations. Specific problems, however, require specific solutions, so Pat has gathered hundreds of useful resources for dealing with your parents' specific circumstances. If your aging parents have a particular difficulty and it is not thoroughly discussed in this volume, you can be sure that she has listed a source—article, book, catalog, tape, or organization—to answer questions and provide assistance.

Pat also reminds you that aging parents can enrich your life with zestful meaning and time-tested wisdom. Your family will seldom regret and never forget the lessons learned in caring for a loved one. Someone who has "seen it all" can help you keep the fast-paced computer age in perspective. Your parents' wisdom and mellowing of many years can help stabilize your teenagers. Learning firsthand about aging and death is the best way for young people to gain appreciation and sensitivity for the elderly.

A registered nurse, Pat is exquisitely sensitive to the emotional turmoil embroiled in your parental relationships. Deep relationships always produce deep feelings—both negative and positive. While helping your aging parent, you may often vacillate between a host of seemingly contradictory emotions, such as love with anger and respect with resentment. These emotional conflicts can devastate and discourage even your most sincere efforts. They may even deeply scar your memories of a loved one. This book offers you a heart-searching and wound-healing analysis of these turbulent emotions.

Because Pat realizes that people have more than just physical and emotional needs, she also emphasizes the importance of nurturing the spiritual needs of our parents. Through faith in the promises of Scripture, elderly believers can look toward the peak of life's tall mountain, with the assurance that as they scale that last treacherous cliff God will transform the flickering light on the distant horizon into the radiant sunshine of a glorious eternity.

Out of this book's many encouraging and practical suggestions swells a hopeful confidence—an attitude that your parents can experience aging as an exciting adventure. By applying the principles in this book, you can enable your parents to truly experience the richness of their "golden years."

Then you can say with them:

> Grow old along with me!
> The best is yet to be,
> The last of life, for which the first was made . . .
> ROBERT BROWNING,
"Rabbi Ben Ezra"

DAVID STERN, M.D.
Coauthor of the revised
None of These Diseases

1

Suddenly They're Older

"When is John coming to see me?" Ellen asked for the fourth time that day.

"Mom," Kathryn explained again, drawing in a deep breath to insure a patient tone, "Dad can't come to see you. He died three years ago. Remember?" She turned to avoid her mother's gaze, a gaze mixed with confusion, doubt, and fear. No, she didn't remember. She couldn't remember.

Then, hoping to distract her mother, Kathryn asked, "Did you enjoy your visit with Jeremy?" Ellen had always enjoyed her teenage grandson.

"Jeremy," she smiled as she repeated the name. Her smile vanished as quickly as the sun behind a storm cloud. "Jeremy never comes to chat with me anymore. Why doesn't he come? No one does. . . ." Her words matched the sharp anger in her eyes.

"Mother," Kathryn continued gently, "Jeremy came by this afternoon. He brought one of his puppies."

"Puppies . . . oh, of course," her voice softened. "But that was so long ago."

In the brief silence, guilt forced itself once more into Kathryn's mind, as it had a dozen times already that day. *Why am I so impatient?* she thought. *I love my mother, and yet there are times . . . times I wish she were gone. I shouldn't think that way. I need to remember she just doesn't understand. I'm forty-eight years old; you'd think I'd have more control—*

Ellen's outburst interrupted her thoughts.

"Where's my lunch? I haven't eaten all day. The doctor said I had to eat right."

"You had lunch, Mother," Kathryn assured. "But if you're hungry I'll bring you a snack." She smiled and bent to kiss her mother's cheek.

"Who are you, Dear?" Ellen asked. "Oh, of course, how silly of me. You're Susan."

Kathryn sighed. "I'm Kathryn, Mother."

"Kathryn, yes." Her eyes cleared for an instant. "Why am I so forgetful? I only have two daughters, you'd think I could keep them straight. Sometimes I think I'm losing my mind. It's a bad feeling, you know, forgetting like this."

Tears clouded Kathryn's eyes. Yes, it was a bad feeling. At sixty-eight, Ellen suffers from *senile dementia.*

Kathryn and her husband brought Ellen into their home two years ago, when her memory lapses and inability to function in her own apartment became increasingly evident. Now Kathryn and her sister, Susan, share the responsibility of caring for their mother. The care she now requires is too heavy a burden for Kathryn alone.

What Can We Do?

Scenes like this one are being repeated over and over again in homes like Kathryn's. When an aging parent needs care, the adult children find themselves caught in a web woven of compassion, love, responsibility, guilt, and fear. Suddenly they're older and we're faced with the questions: What can we do? How can we help?

As a registered nurse I see numerous cases where families bring their aging parents home. The extended family care provides an atmosphere of belonging and love.

Unfortunately, not everyone is able to bring their parent home. Some aging parents require more extensive care than the family can offer within the home.

This happened in my family. My grandmother was eventually placed in a nursing home, when her adult children could no longer care for her in their homes.

Grandma, a diabetic, had become incontinent and could no longer care for herself. She needed continuous medical care. Her family, after much deliberation, decided the nursing home would be the best course to follow.

While many of the elderly require some degree of care, fortunately, many more aging parents prefer and are quite capable of managing on their own, living either independently or semi-independently.

Semi-Independent and Loving It

Uncle Gunder, for example, lives in a small home next to his daughter Marian and her family. When Gunder's wife Selma had a stroke several years ago, Marian became concerned about her parents living alone. Since Marian and her husband had just built a new house on their lakefront property, they invited Gunder and Selma to live in the home they had vacated.

Selma died fifteen years ago and Gunder, now ninety-three, still lives in that home. He tends three gardens, cleans house, cooks his meals—except for dinner—feeds the animals, and sees to his personal needs. In fact, he manages to keep up with the news in his own native country, Norway, as well as with what's happening in the rest of the world.

A nearby home or apartment, this family believes, is an excellent way to help their aging parent maintain independence. At the same time the family remains close by, should help be needed.

There are many alternatives in choosing the type of facility suitable for your aging parent. We'll explore those possibilities a little later in the book. But first let's take a look at what constitutes an aging parent.

How Old Is an Aging Parent?

At ninety-six Uncle Gunder can be classified as an aging parent. But, chronological age has nothing to do with determining when parents may need their family's help.

For example, my friend Sarah admits, "I had never thought Mom might ever be dependent. She's only fifty years old."

For most of us, fifty is still an age that boasts independence. Yet, unfortunately, a year ago, Sarah's mother, Martha, suffered a stroke which left her an invalid. She moved from a happy, industrious, self-sufficient life into the frustrating, and at times devastating, realm of total dependence.

Sarah had to face early on questions that many of us will encounter as our parents grow older: What to do and how to help?

"For me there was no question," Sarah said, "I had to bring her home. After all, who's more qualified to care for her? I love her, and I'm a registered nurse."

Sarah cares for her mother and continues to work at her job in the hospital. However, she admits, "I can't leave Martha alone for more than three to four hours at a time, so I'll need to hire someone to come in and sit with her when I'm gone."

Since Sarah is single and a registered nurse, the decision was not as difficult for her as it might be for others. Most families have limited time, and little nursing knowledge. Many also have limited housing facilities.

Each situation varies, but with most people, there is a common denominator—we care. When our aging parents need us, whether it is to help them make minor adjustments or arrange for complete care, we want to help.

The Generational Sandwich

For many adult children, the problems of caring for our aging parents may come at a time when we are deparenting our own youngsters, brooding over an empty nest, struggling with menopause and mid-life crisis. We are sandwiched between generations.

One side of the bread is young and often fresh. Our kids are just finishing school, or beginning careers and families of their own. Many times they still need us.

The other side of the bread is older, firm, but at times dry, brittle, and easily broken. Our parents who once saw to all our needs and took responsibility for us, now may have to look to us for help and support.

We—the butter and meat—are sandwiched in the middle. Did anyone ever tell you you were full of bologna? Well, now you can tell them you *are* the bologna—or the salami, or the liverwurst. More simply, we are the wage earners, the responsibility factor that holds the generational sandwich together.

So Where Do We Start?

It's obvious then, since we are the ones most likely to inherit the responsibility of seeing to the health and welfare of our parents, that we must prepare and equip ourselves for the task.

Where do we start?

When you enter any project or program, one of the first steps is to determine your skill level. Say, for example, you were to enter a nursing program. As a nursing student your goal would be to learn all you could about people and the medical care you would eventually be responsible for.

You are about to enter a program in which you will learn how to become a care-giver in order to help and care for your aging parents. Let's proceed by assessing your skill level. In chapter 2 you'll find a series of questions relating to the elderly and their care. The quiz and its answers will increase your knowledge of the aging process.

Later, we'll evaluate emotions such as guilt, anger, or resentment and learn how to deal with them and improve family relationships. Throughout the book you'll find practical helps and uplifting answers to the countless questions adult children may encounter in caring for aging parents.

You'll have the help you need to find the most appropriate and safest environment. You'll find hope in the inspirational and uplifting stories and thoughts, and you'll develop the ability to cope as we share each other's burdens, pains, and pleasures along the way.

2

Aging's Just Another Word for Growing Up

In the moment of birth we begin the journey to the end of life.

How much do you know about growing old? Maybe you're thinking, *I don't really want to know about aging. I'm learning too fast as it is.*

Even if we don't want to learn about aging, we will in time, so why not gain that knowledge now, before winter catches us unprepared and it's too late to exercise any control? Besides, by being aware of the aging process, we are better able to help our parents, as well as ourselves, age more graciously and intelligently.

You can test your aging awareness level by answering the following questions. Some of the answers may surprise you.

Aging Awareness Test

	True	False
1. Senility or senile dementia is a normal part of body breakdown in the aging process.	☐	☐
2. Senile dementia is irreversible.	☐	☐
3. After the age of sixty-five the ability to learn is greatly diminished.	☐	☐
4. Creativity diminishes with age.	☐	☐
5. Most older people are physically weak and in poor health.	☐	☐

True   False

6. Over 50 percent of elderly people need nursing home or similar type care.   □   □
7. Vision loss or change is noted in over half of the people over sixty-five.   □   □
8. In the aging process, people's senses become less acute.   □   □
9. Only about one-third of the population over sixty suffer from hearing loss.   □   □
10. Retirement seems to bring about declining health.   □   □
11. Older people are unable to adjust to modern innovations.   □   □
12. The aging process causes people to become more self-absorbed and uninterested in community affairs.   □   □
13. Most elderly people have little or no interest in sexual activity.   □   □
14. Sexual capabilities diminish rapidly after sixty-five years of age.   □   □
15. Sixty-five percent of America's elderly are below poverty level or in economic straits.   □   □

Answers: 1. F; 2. F; 3. F; 4. F; 5. F; 6. F; 7. T; 8. T; 9. T; 10. F; 11. F; 12. F; 13. F; 14. F.; 15. F.

How did you do? Seven or more correct answers gives you a passing score. What happens if you failed? Relax. You'll simply have to go back to Aging Basics, and shuffle down the hall for a few hours in Grandma's slippers. Even if you passed and can enter the course at Aging Awareness—Level 1, I'm sure you'll want to join in and learn more about the aging process to better understand and provide better care for your aging parent.

The Myths and Realities of Aging

Now, back to the true and false of aging. Take a look at the first statement. *Senility or senile dementia is a normal part of body breakdown....* The answer? *False.* Are you surprised?

Actually, the whole phrase is wrong. When most people see the word *senility*, their negative brain waves flash in "forgetfulness" or "dementia" as a fact of old age. However, senility and dementia have entirely different meanings.

A Long and Happy Senility to All?

Defining terms. *Senility:* "Old age. The sum of physical and mental changes occurring in advanced life." (Latin root: to grow old.) All of us experience senility. Now we can wish each other a long and happy senility. Right?

Dementia: "Global impairment of cognition, personality, and behavior, which may be reversible." (Latin root: deprived of mind.) Thankfully, dementia does not always accompany age.

As you can see, the two are very different. According to a recent article in a local newspaper, "These (referring to forgetfulness and other symptoms of senile dementia) are not the inexorable signs of advancing age. They may be the mark of a serious illness: Alzheimer's disease." Another article stated, "Emotional problems and physical maladies may cause families to believe their elder to be 'senile.' "

The second statement on the Aging Awareness Test, *Senile dementia is irreversible*, is also false. Since symptoms similar to those found in senile dementia can be traced to physical or emotional problems, and even to medications, those symptoms can be relieved.

Take Mary's case for example. At seventy-five, Mary had been growing increasingly forgetful and confused. Her concerned daughter, Carol, realized her mother needed extra care.

Problem 1: A drug supply large enough to establish her own pharmacy. Carol counted dozens of medicine bottles in Mary's cupboard, many of them outdated and some duplicates. Carol confronted her mother in an effort to clarify which medications she actually needed, and tried to establish the what, when, where, why, and how of this drug cache.

Problem 2: Too many doctors. After an hour of, "Dr. Star gave me the pink pills. They're for my blood pressure. Dr. Allen prescribed the white pills for my heart and the red ones for my arthritis. Dr. White said I could take those big yellow ones to help me sleep and the red capsules to keep me 'regular,' and those little yellow ones are for my 'nerves'. . . ." Carol counted eleven medications prescribed by five different doctors to cover everything from gout to constipation.

Carol immediately made an appointment with Dr. Andrews, her mother's current M.D., for Mary to have a physical exam. All the medications were brought in and lined up for the doctor's verdict.

A few muttered oaths later, Dr. Andrews calmed down and advised Carol of a plan to wean Mary from all medication so she could be properly evaluated.

Within a few weeks, Mary's symptoms of senility disappeared. She proved to be in excellent health, needing only two of the previously prescribed medications.

Dr. Andrews had said, "Mary, I don't know how you managed to survive. Most of us would be in our graves if we'd downed such a mixture of medication."

You Can't Teach an Old Dog New Tricks—Or Can You?

Let's move on to statement number 3: *After the age of sixty-five the ability to learn is greatly diminished.*

Is it? Let me introduce some seniors who would disagree.

"Age puzzles me. I thought it was a quiet time. My seventies were interesting, and fairly serene; but my eighties were passionate. I grow more intense as I age. To my own surprise I burst out with hot conviction" (Florida Scott Maxwell, *The Measure of My Days*).

Eighty-eight-year-old author, Helen Santmyer, began her novel in 1920. She worked from 1976 on revising . . . *And Ladies of the Club,* which was released in 1982 and immediately became a best-seller. Helen resides in a nursing home and suffers from emphysema.

According to the January 1984 *Guideposts* magazine, Jessie Ryan earned her high school diploma at age ninety-eight. "What's more," she said, "I'm taking classes next year, and I'm going to learn all I can."

Creativity diminishes with age? To that I hope you gave a resounding, *"False!"* Learning and creativity go hand in hand. In fact, many people don't discover their created purpose until their winter years. Then instead of winter they celebrate the harvest. Do you know of any late bloomers? Or people whose creativity outlives them?

Grandma Moses began her career in art at seventy years of age and was still painting at age 101.

Michelangelo died at age ninety while in the process of redesigning St. Peter's Church.

George Burns, at eighty, won an Oscar for his role in *The Sunshine Boys*. Since then he has embarked on a new career as an author. George claims, "I've made old age fashionable."

A local paper recently reported, "Massive amounts of research show that the human brain, unless diseased or damaged, does not deteriorate with age in any crucial way." The article went on to say, "The usual mental losses not associated with disease are due most often to social and psychological impacts. Those who withdraw from life, reduce their mental activities or fail to seek new experiences account for the fact some old people do poorly while others retain their faculties quite well. . . ."

Have you, like me, been thinking all this time that our brain cells are dying every year? You'll be happy to know we were wrong. The latest studies indicate that the greatest cell loss occurs in early life and the cells lost later are insignificant.

That's good news not only for us adult children who are growing older, but for our aging parents as well. Keeping alert and active can make a difference. As any fitness fan will testify, exercise helps get oxygen to the brain, thereby increasing mental awareness.

Although my research tells me mental and physical activity don't protect against diseases that involve the brain, it is encouraging to know that of those sixty-five and older, only 5 percent may suffer some dementia. The percentage increases by about 1 percentile per year of age. I'll share more about the various illnesses that affect the elderly in chapters 8 and 9.

Now that we've discredited the myth about decreasing intelligence and senility among older persons, let's discover what happens to the body. Do we really fall apart?

Slowing Down Doesn't Mean STOP

Take a look at statement 5, *Most older people are physically weak and in poor health.* At one time I would have answered "True." However, as I researched aging, I found some pleasantly surprising statistics that give me hope for my parents and myself.

While health problems do increase among the elderly population, most can still continue regular activities. Many—especially today, with our emphasis on sports—continue to maintain excellent physical condition.

Recently, while watching the winter Olympics, a young man of 108, "Jack Rabbit" (Herman) Johansen, told us that he cross-country skis every day. He did admit to slowing down some; he can't compete like he used to. Mr. Johansen lives in Canada and is a member of the Cross-Country Hall of Fame.

Duncan MacLean, at the age of ninety, won a silver medal at the 1975 World Veterans' Olympics in Canada. He ran 200 meters in forty-four seconds. His goal at that time? "To run 100 meters on my hundredth birthday."

While not every elderly person will indulge in strenuous physical activity, only about 5 percent require nursing home or other institutional type care.

Although physical limitations develop naturally with age, the majority are not weak or in poor health.

"... the Dust Returns to the Earth ..."

What about vision loss in more than half the people over sixty-five? Do people's senses become less acute with age?

One of the most vivid accounts of the degeneration of the body was written by King Solomon. His words are recorded in the Bible in Ecclesiastes 12.

> ... the keepers of the house tremble (limbs), and the strong men are bent (legs), and the grinders cease because they are few (teeth), and those that look through the windows are dimmed (eyes), and the doors on the street are shut; when the sound of the grinding is low (hearing loss), and one rises up at the voice of a bird (insomnia), and all the daughters of song are brought low (tuneless, quivering voice); they are afraid also of what is high, and terrors are in the way

(fear of heights and falling); the almond tree blossoms
(white-haired), the grasshopper drags itself along (slow) and
desire fails, because man goes to his eternal home, and the
mourners go about the streets; . . . (vv. 3–5).

These verses are a plea to remember God, our Creator, before it is
too late, because eventually, ". . . dust returns to the earth as it was,
and the spirit returns to God who gave it" (v. 7).

I encourage you not to look upon the degeneration of the physical
body as depressing. Aging should be a celebration, with growing an-
ticipation that each day brings us closer to God. It is a growing up or
maturing into the people God created us to be.

Turning It Off Versus Getting It On

Does retirement bring about declining health?   No. That is, it
shouldn't unless a person takes retirement literally and ceases to function. Most active elderly people don't retire, they just change profes-
sions and priorities. We'll learn more on the importance of remaining
active in a later chapter.

How do the elderly adjust to all the newfangled technology?   Can
they adjust? When you consider the elderly of today and the changes
that have occurred in their lifetime, you have to laugh at that question.

My parents and grandparents lived in a farming community in
North Dakota. Their transportation consisted of a horse and buggy in
the summer and horse and sleigh in the winter. When the auto came
along, they adjusted to the change. Aerotechnology, wars, economic
depression, and the computer age have all transpired in their life-
times.

According to Dave Ammons in a recent newspaper article, "Their
very survival shows ability to change. Seniors may choose the routine
and the familiar because it's comfortable, but that is different from inability to change" (*The Columbian*).

**Does the aging process cause people to become more self-absorbed
and uninterested in community affairs?**   No. In addition to doing a

vast majority of volunteer work and having heavy community involvement, elders tend to have a high voting rate. They are, for the most part interested in the economic and political scenes locally, nationally, and worldwide.

Is Sex for Seniors?

Would you be embarrassed or surprised to find out your seventy-eight-year-old mother and her new husband, eighty-two, were sexually active?

Somehow, we mistakenly believe that sex is for the young, when in fact, "even at seventy and up, only a minority say they have little or no interest." So says an article in the March 1984 issue of *Reader's Digest*. Their information is based on a survey and book called *Love, Sex, and Aging: A Consumers Union Report* by Edward M. Brecher and the editors of Consumer Report Books.

The report also indicates that, "even beyond seventy, over half of the women and three-quarters of the men are still interested in sex."

One eighty-three-year-old woman commented, "Younger readers will thank you for giving them hope for their old age. Older readers will thank you for bringing their feelings and actions out of the closet."

Guideposts, February 1984, tells of a couple from Santiago, Chile, who plan to be married in March. The courtship began after Jose Landeros saw Rosa Chamorro's picture in a newspaper. He called, arranged to meet her, and proposed—all in the same day. Sound romantic? You bet. Jose is 103, and Rosa, 107.

"Many waters cannot quench love, neither can floods drown it" (Song of Solomon 8:7). While the sex drive diminishes eventually in most people, for many, the need for sexual activity continues through a very old age. Our knowledge of this and other facts we've covered in discussing the quiz will help us to better understand and help our parents and ourselves through the aging process.

The Poverty of Age

When you think of old age, what picture comes to mind? Do you see a bent, wrinkled, white-haired woman in a tattered cardigan, starving in her poorly heated apartment? Do you see a bald, frail man with trembling hands, opening a can of dog food for nourishment because people food is too expensive? Do you see elderly couples malnourished from lack of nutritional foods?

In a recent article in our local newspaper, *The Columbian,* this statement appeared: "A recent Louis Harris poll found that 'on every issue tested, the elderly are perceived as being in much more desperate shape than they actually are.'" Appoximately 10 percent of our senior citizens are below poverty level, while another 15 percent are having financial problems. This leaves 75 percent who are doing okay.

This seemed a little low to me—after all how can anyone survive on Social Security checks? In another study done among the elderly by the National Council on Aging, only 15 percent listed "not having enough money to live on" as a major problem. Another facet to this study indicated that the majority of these poor had always suffered economically.

In yet another source, *Common Sense,* by A. L. Williams, the author says, "Most Americans will retire in poverty. According to a recent Census Bureau survey 87% of Americans 65 or older were living on a meager income of less than $10,000." Williams refers to the U.S. Census Bureau Report, 1980, Census of Population and Housing.

After further research, I came up with an article from *U.S. News & World Report,* August 29, 1983, which states, "America's elderly, long assumed to be among the nation's poorest and in need of government help, turn out to have higher incomes than most people." This finding was disclosed by the Census Bureau on August 17, 1983. This was the bureau's first-ever study of after-tax income. The reason for this change, the article reports, is that the elderly pay the smallest share of their incomes to taxes.

Isn't it just like the government to add to the confusion with all these statistics? The stats still haven't given us a straight answer and probably never will. The best we can do is to take a look at the people around us. How are they doing?

Most of the older people I know are managing okay. None of them are wealthy, but they aren't destitute either. Of course, I've seen many elderly folks manage very well on fairly low incomes. I suppose it's because many of them survived the depression years and learned by experience how to live on practically nothing.

Finances and how you can help your aging parent are another area we'll talk about in more detail later.

Our main objective in this chapter has been to dispel some of the myths about aging and get some ideas as to what really happens when people age.

These facts can give us better understanding of our role as caregivers to our aging parents. Before we go on to the next chapter, I have a confession.

Before I began my research on aging, I had a lot of wrong ideas. Like so many people on the down side of fifty, I thought life, for the most part, just stopped, or at least slowed down to a slug's pace, when you got old. I looked at the elderly as being unable. Unable, that is, to do practically anything.

Let's just say that the reality of aging turned out to be the opposite in many ways of what I originally thought. Aging Basics has given me a whole new attitude about the aging process and taught me some important facts I needed to know in caring for aging parents.

Why am I telling you this? I guess I just don't want you to feel guilty over what you didn't know. And, speaking of guilt, in this next chapter you'll find a quiz that gets into feelings we have toward our aging parents—and those feelings aren't always love and devotion. We'll learn how to resolve those negative emotions that threaten our family relationships.

3

Emotions

"I've never felt so helpless, so hurt, so . . . desolate in my whole life." John, aged forty-one, shares the pain of emotional conflict in dealing with his father, a victim of *Alzheimer's disease.*

"Dad had wet himself, and when I suggested a bath, he refused and became extremely agitated. Every time I tried to help him, he pushed me away. I finally ended up wrestling him to the floor to change him. He started crying. I felt—I don't know—angry, hopeless, scared. How do you find words to describe a scene like that? All I know is I wanted Dad to hold me and protect me like he used to.

"Instead, my dad, this stranger, is sprawled out on the floor, crying and getting his diaper changed like a two-year-old. My dad, the guy who taught me how to fish, and hunt, to build . . . He built this house . . . he. . . ." John paused to brush the tears away.

Composed again, John continued. "In that moment, I became the father, and my dad, the little kid. I wasn't ready for it. I don't suppose anyone ever could be. Things like that just happen. Suddenly, you know you have to take over. Dad will never be a parent to me again. The roles have changed. It's a fact, but facts don't take away the pain or make this damnable disease any easier to cope with."

Like John, finding yourself in the middle of a role change, where you become the care-giver, is like thrashing through an emotional jungle. Amidst the trees of love and tenderness, and vines of generosity, concern, and devotion flourishes an undergrowth of anger, hostility, resentment, dread, helplessness, shame, and guilt.

In order to be effective care-givers, we must learn to cope with these emotions. As you read through the next few pages, you'll learn to understand and better cope with the feelings of the elderly. Then we'll move into the realm of your own feelings, and how you can accept them, understand them, and finally, take action to deal with them if necessary.

How Does It Feel to Grow Old?

One of the first steps in caring for aging parents is to gain empathy for them. That is, to understand how it feels to grow old, to face up to our parents' and our own mortality.

To a few, old age declares a battle won, a celebration, a promise of rest. For many, there is fear and resentment. Some become bitter and angry. Some try so diligently not to grow old, that when old age hits with the icy fingered grasp of a blizzard, they turn inside themselves in shame and self-pity.

Old age *is not* shameful, nor is it a condition to be pitied. Yet in our youth-oriented society, for many, growing old has become a nightmare. People have many and varied feelings about aging. We'll openly explore how you feel about your own aging, and then how you feel about your aging parents so that you might better understand yourself and them in order to offer the best help and care possible.

Sometimes I'm Afraid

Are you afraid of growing old? Sometimes I am. Not that I fear losing my youthful figure. I lost the battle of the bulge ages ago; now I'm just holding my ground. I look forward to growing older so I can be a soft grandma. I loved my soft grandma.

Nor am I afraid of gray hair. I proudly bare the few I have as a shining crown of honor, adding sparkle to my naturally brown tresses. I doubt I'll cover the gray. Grandma had gray hair. No, not really gray, but strands of silver, braided and beautiful.

And wrinkles? They're coming. They represent proof of my laughter, and a smile I hope will never fade away.

Poor health? Like most people I'm sometimes afraid that perhaps someday I will be one of the few elderly with senile dementia, crippling arthritis, or other physical problems. I fear the possibility of being dependent on others with no mind of my own. And yet, why fear such a remote possibility? There is a higher risk of being permanently injured in an auto accident as I drive the expressway.

What then? Do I fear death? No. I know death will bring me peace and reunion with God.

But *I am* afraid when I see that, in our culture, we value aged wine and antiques more than aging people. Isn't it true that the older a vase or piece of furniture, the more adulation it receives? It is placed on a shelf of honor. Because a thing has survived the years and trials of life it is respected and even revered.

In our society, as people grow older, respect slips away. When "youthfulness" then "usefulness" subside, many elderly are shuffled aside and forgotten.

We look to antiques, relics, and archeological digs to give us answers to the past. But, we forget some of our most valuable resources. We close our ears to these human vessels, brimming with scenes of yesterday, filled with a lifetime of wisdom and knowledge. So often, instead of offering the elderly a place of honor, and listening to their tales, we tend to label their murmurings of the past "senile," and lock their memories away in cobwebbed attics.

Is it any wonder that we often admit, "Yes, I am afraid of growing old."

Many feelings accompany aging. Those fears I listed above account for a wide variety of emotions. But the most common emotion, and probably the most difficult one for us to understand, is grief.

The Grief of Old Age

Grief isn't just mourning over the death of a loved one. Grief may be experienced if any part of the body ceases to function. The loss of a limb, loss of hearing, eyesight, even the excision of a tumor, brings an ache known as grief. Then, of course, there are the exterior losses of job, home, personal possessions, income, and loss of a spouse or friends.

The natural process of mourning brings feelings of guilt, anger, despair, denial, depression, then hopefully acceptance. The trouble is, with aging, sometimes the losses come so steadily, the older person is in a constant state of unresolved grief.

This unresolved grief or sense of loss often shows up in the form of physical complaints, manipulative cries for attention, denial of limitations, and placing the blame for their problems on others.

Older people face the fear of rejection, loneliness, illness, and death. Some fear poverty and homelessness. Many feel guilt and anxiety over becoming a burden to their adult children.

Although we can't take away our parents' hurts, we can help them cope, and encourage them. It's such a relief just to know someone cares and understands.

Feelings

Adult children often suffer grief themselves as they face the dilemma of how and where the aging parent should be cared for. We, too, suffer loss as our parents change, and the same grieving process hits us. We may find ourselves wandering though the middle of that emotional jungle, with our feelings ranging from love to hate, and from compassion to resentment toward our parents, ourselves, and our changing roles. Is it any wonder we get confused?

I did say we were going to explore emotions and ourselves. The time has come to dig deep inside and find out how you really feel about your aging parent(s).

The quiz below is designed not to test you, but to make you aware of your own emotions. Please be honest in your answers. Remember, no one is going to see them but you. Your answers should reflect the way you *really* feel, not the way you wish you felt.

The Emotional Side of Aging

1. How would you best describe the feelings you have toward your aging parent(s)? (Check more than one if necessary.)
   Compassion ☐ Love ☐ Respect ☐ Sadness ☐ Tenderness ☐
   Indifference ☐ Anger ☐ Resentment ☐ Helplessness ☐ Guilt ☐
2. Do you often feel confused about conflicting emotions?
   Yes ☐ No ☐

3. How do you best remember your parent(s) as you were growing up?

   Mother: _____

   Father: _____

   (For example: "My father expected a lot from me—somehow I always felt I couldn't measure up to his expectations." "My mother always cared for us. I can't remember a time when I needed her that she wasn't there.")

4. If your response to question 3 was negative, have you ever resolved your areas of conflict? Yes ☐ No ☐

5. Do you ever feel resentment toward your parent(s) for their growing dependence on you? Yes ☐ No ☐

6. Do you ever experience bitterness, contempt, or hostility toward your parent(s)? Yes ☐ No ☐

7. Are you unexplainably fearful or anxious around your aging parent(s)? Yes ☐ No ☐

8. Are you ashamed of your parent(s)? Yes ☐ No ☐ Or embarrassed to take them to a public place? Yes ☐ No ☐

9. Do you find your patience frequently growing thin where your aging parent(s) is concerned? Yes ☐ No ☐

10. Do you ever feel like closing your eyes and walking away from any responsibility you might have toward your elderly parent(s)? Yes ☐ No ☐

11. Can you accept the physical and/or mental deterioration of your aging parent(s)? Yes ☐ No ☐

12. Do you like your aging parent(s)? Yes ☐ No ☐

13. Can you accept aging in yourself? Yes ☐ No ☐

14. Are you afraid of death? For your parent(s)? Yes ☐ No ☐ For yourself? Yes ☐ No ☐

15. Do you feel that caring for an aging parent(s) in addition to your many other responsibilities becomes too heavy a load at times? Yes ☐ No ☐

16. Do you often feel guilty about your attitude or relationship with your aging parent(s)? Yes ☐ No ☐

Heavy wasn't it? As I indicated before, this is not a test, but rather a search to find your real feelings.

Mixed Up? Congratulations—You're Normal

If you recognized some or all of these feelings interwoven in the relationship between you and your parent, congratulations. You are very human—and normal.

You probably didn't mind confessing to those positive emotions such as love, compassion, respect, and tenderness. We welcome such feelings and cherish our ability to have them. But what about resentment, bitterness, guilt, anger, hatred? Those we're *not* so happy about. But we need to remember that the deeper our commitment to someone, the deeper the feelings go—all feelings.

Take the relationship between a husband and wife, for instance; one minute it's like you're on your honeymoon, and the next you could be spouting off at each other with the violence of Mount Vesuvius. Why? Because everything a spouse says or does affects you. Why? Because the love is so intense.

In much the same way, it is quite natural for us to feel a tea-warm tenderness for a parent one moment and a lava-hot anger the next.

My friend Renee admits, "It's a frustrating situation, but one that happens. Everything might be going along fine. Then suddenly, Mom makes a comment. It can be about anything, from an innocent comment like, 'The soup is too cold,' to a guilt-producing statement such as, 'You're not going out again tonight, are you?' And I stomp out of the house like a rebellious kid, muttering, 'I'm not going to be manipulated.'

"Sometimes," Renee says, "the anger isn't from anything she says, but from my own frustrations or inadequacies."

"Be Angry But Do Not Sin ..."

All of the emotions we feel from time to time are normal. It is the way we deal with them that can cause problems. While it's okay for Renee to become very angry with her mother, it would be wrong for her to express that anger to or direct it toward her invalid mother. At the same time it may be just as harmful to hold the anger in and let it build.

"So," you may be asking, "what do I do with my anger—suppress it?"

Sometimes it's necessary to suppress the anger initially. If you must release your anger, step outside and yell at your hibiscus. Or get in the car and scream, pound on the piano, vacuum the carpet, or kill your pillow.

It's okay to get angry—even God allows that in us. The Bible tells us, "Be angry but do not sin; do not let the sun go down on your anger" (Ephesians 4:26).

So get rid of the anger and those feelings that could lead to more serious relationship-hurting explosions every day—before the sun goes down. The idea is to work through potential problems before they can erupt into a full-blown storm. As my pastor explains it, "The apostle Paul is imploring his listeners to make a daily accounting of things that have the potential of making mountains out of molehills."

"... What I Don't Want to Do I Do ..."

None of us wants to erupt in anger, or hoard feelings of resentment or bitterness. Yet how often we repeat the words of the apostle Paul, "For that which I am doing, I do not understand; for I am not practicing what I would like to do, but I am doing the very thing I hate" (Romans 7:15 NAS).

Part of the conflict comes from our own confusion between feelings and intellect. For example, intellectually, I know that my parent needs care and I am willing to give it. The decision to become a caregiver is made based on my ability, my relationship with my parent, and other circumstances.

Emotions are seldom thought out beforehand. Most of us wouldn't arbitrarily say, "Tomorrow at 2:00 A.M., Dad is going to wake up and demand to go home, insisting he's been kidnapped, and I'm going to be angry."

Rather, emotions come and go like thunderstorms, with little or no warning. Oh, sometimes the warning signs are out, but we don't always see them until it's too late. Then we're caught in the storm and end up having to say, "I'm sorry."

Anger is only one of the many emotions that seem to surface with the changes that occur as our parents grow older and become more dependent on us.

Another friend, Judy, commented, "Sometimes I have so much love and compassion, I feel like I can handle anything. My generosity overwhelms me. Then there are days I think, *Why me?*

"The other day, for instance, I was getting ready for church and went in to check on Mom. She had been incontinent and had gotten diarrheal stool all over herself.

"I felt angry, resentful, sorry for myself, and probably a few other things I can't say out loud, all at the same time. After I changed clothes and mumbled about how I couldn't even go to church, I gathered a basin of water, washcloths, and towels and trudged in to do a chore no one, least of all me, should be saddled with.

"She had stool everywhere, even between her toes and under her toenails. Oh, I did my job admirably; I even assured her it was okay. I had just about finished cleaning her up and had placed her feet in the basin when it happened.

"A picture appeared in my mind of Jesus washing the feet of the disciples. I knew it was God's way of showing me what a lousy attitude I had. Instead of meeting her needs with a servant's heart, I had grudgingly set out to do the hated task, thinking, *Why me? I was made for better things.*

"I had been so concerned with my own discomfort I hadn't even thought of the humiliation my mother felt. This time when I looked into her hurt and pain-filled eyes I could reassure her that it really was okay and that I still loved her.

"Even though I realize that the negative emotions I get from time to time are valid and normal, I know sometimes I take them too far, and God shows me I need to deal with them by asking forgiveness."

In her book, *Home Care—An Alternative to the Nursing Home,* Florine DeFresne shares the emotional response involved in the decision to care for her husband at home. She says, "Our humanity doesn't disappear because we are trying to be super caregivers . . . I did not always keep a calm spirit. Sometimes my patience was stretched to the limit . . . I had to learn to accept me."

You will have come a long way in dealing with emotions when you learn to accept them. Accept them, yes, but don't let them carry you into trouble. The next step in solving the problems caused by emotional conflicts is understanding why the emotions crop up in the first place.

"I Feel Guilty (Resentful, Angry) Because ..."

It's not too difficult to understand why Judy felt all that emotional turmoil when she walked into her mother's room just as she was leaving for church. How would you feel?

Some people today would tell Judy she should have smiled immediately and said, "PRAISE THE LORD!" I'm sorry, but I can't buy that philosophy, at least not totally. It's just plain unnatural. The key word here though is *immediately*. Understand that emotions do come on suddenly, often without warning. Immediate response is usually not the same as a well thought out one would be.

Judy's final response was one of thankfulness and joy. Through the experience Judy learned about the importance of a servant attitude. And she saw how the experience had hurt her mother far more than it had hurt her.

Let's take a look at another example of the why of emotions.

Some emotional problems between the adult child and aging parent are not so easily explained. Bob felt guilty about the relationship he had with his father.

"I don't understand it," Bob confessed, "I take good care of Dad, see that all his needs are met, yet I feel guilty. It's to the point where I'm uncomfortable around him all the time. I'm feeling more and more depressed and frustrated. At times I can't cope at all, and that only increases the problem."

After some counseling, Bob found his overwhelming load of negative feelings were due to unresolved conflicts from his adolescence. Bob always felt his Dad expected more of him than he could give.

He admits, "I could never be the kid I thought my dad wanted. I always felt he expected me to be the perfect image of himself and I couldn't live up to his expectations. Finally, I started lying to him about achievements I hadn't really earned so he'd be proud of me."

Once Bob understood the root of the problem, he could begin to resolve the conflict and eliminate much of the emotional turmoil involved in caring for his aging father.

If you think that one was complicated, you're right. But not nearly as complicated as some cases. It is important to understand why certain negative emotions plague you, especially if they produce conflicts that lead to disunity or broken relationships, or even threaten your sanity.

Bob's guilt created a deep wedge between him and his father. He finally sought counseling for the depression, which really wasn't the root of the problem at all. But through the symptom of depression he was able to get down to the real hurt, an unresolved conflict—a root of bitterness, covered with guilt which had grown into a tangled emotional mess.

Finding Solutions

Understanding negative emotions is important. When those emotions run beyond your understanding, professional help may be needed. This is the third area of dealing with emotions—taking action and finding solutions.

For some, a deeper understanding of the whys of emotions may be found in books such as *Emotionally Free* by Rita Bennett. They often provide better understanding of unresolved conflicts and may help you attain an attitude of forgiveness as you go through a healing process.

Janet, a close friend, had been the victim of sexual abuse by her father.

Another, Annette, could never understand her feelings of being unwanted. Finally, she learned that her mother had been raped and she was the product of that hateful act. The man she'd always known as "Dad" had never really accepted her.

Kathy went through inner healing therapy to deal with the hate she felt toward both her father and mother. She hated her father for the way he physically abused her mother and his open affection for other women. She hated her mother for her weakness in allowing it to happen.

Although most of our parental relationships are not this serious, many of us have experienced some sort of conflict with our parents. Forgiveness is the key we must turn in order to release ourselves from the hold that negative emotions can have over us. The emotional turmoil that often emerges as we deal with our aging parents can leave us bewildered, depressed, and guilt ridden. Trying to find all the answers as to the who, what, where, when, and why of emotions may be like chasing a rainbow.

I think I can safely say we have learned to accept our emotions as normal. And, I hope you have gained a better understanding of the emotional process, and why it plagues us. Now we come to the final stage in dealing with emotions—taking action.

In other words, we move on to solve the problem and seek help on the way if necessary.

"I've Got to Talk to Somebody"

It's obvious that when our feelings overpower us and cause us to act out inappropriately or threaten our sanity, we need help. Our action is to seek professional help.

But what if you are still operating within normally sane limits and you just need a little help now and then?

Say you can accept your emotions and understand why they come. You don't suffer from unresolved conflicts and you really don't need professional help. But, if you don't vent your hostilities you'll go crazy as a fox in a hound's pen.

"I've got to talk to somebody," you cry.

It's obvious that we can't vent our anger and frustrations on our elderly parents, so what do we do? Remember what you did to vent your emotions when dealing with small children who didn't understand you, or teenagers whom *you* didn't understand? I remember very well what I did. I talked to other parents in the same patched up life raft. We shared frustrations and pains. We shared each other's troubles and burdens. It worked well then, why not now?

Many of you may feel uncomfortable about turning to friends in troubled times, especially when the trouble is with your aging parent. But this is no different from any other crisis. You need to know you are not alone. You need the support and encouragement of others.

One woman whose husband has Alzheimer's said, "Before I joined a support group, I thought our family was the only one to have problems like this. It's been a real blessing to have people who actually understand and that you can laugh with and cry with."

Because there are still people in the world who don't understand, stick with those who do. Your deepest sharing times should be with comrades who suffer similar problems and who have empathy, not just sympathy. There is a difference. (For information on additional helps and support groups see chapter 14.)

A support system can do wonders in helping you cope as you make your way through that emotional jungle. It can even help waylay those guilt feelings that seem to come in and weigh you down even when you don't think you've done anything wrong.

And speaking of guilt, we haven't really resolved it yet, have we?

Since guilt seems to be the most prominent emotion in people with aging parents, I've decided to dedicate the whole next chapter to uncovering guilt, explaining it, and getting rid of it.

4

Guilt

Guilt can be a devastating emotion.

It is also the emotion that most frequently tears down relationships between parent and child, so I'd like to offer a solution for handling guilt that has helped me tremendously. Perhaps it can help you as well.

A Guilt by Any Other Name

Not long ago, I wrote a book called *Have You Hugged Your Teenager Today?* In it, I discussed at length the whys and wherefores of parental guilt as it relates to living with teenagers. Even though I concentrated on the parent–teen relationship, I've found that the same principles apply in nearly all relationships. Even though the circumstances may change, guilt is still guilt and can be handled in much the same way.

The first step is to break guilt into two categories, *true* guilt and *false* guilt. I know you'll be overjoyed at this revelation, but, some of the guilt we experience is real. It is brought on by some wrongdoing, whether in our actions or attitude.

Freedom From Guilt Is Easy When It's Real

As I searched for logical and helpful solutions to cancel my own guilt trips, I found the most freeing principles in God's word.

40

True guilt is what the Bible calls "Godly or constructive sorrow." It is a guilt or sadness in us that makes us want to change our behavior. True guilt works as a signal to tell us we've done wrong and should take steps to make amends.

It reminds me of a story I once heard. A man came in to see the doctor. "Doc," the patient grimaced as he flexed his knee, "it hurts when I do this."

"Well then," the doctor replied, "don't do that."

I'll agree, the doctor's cure was rather simplistic, but eliminating true guilt can be that simple. Amazingly enough, true guilt is the best kind to have because it is so easy to get rid of. God has promised us release in this way: "If we confess our sins, he is faithful and just, and will forgive our sins and cleanse us from all unrighteousness" (1 John 1:9).

We can't always keep from doing wrong. Often we find ourselves having to say, "I'm sorry." Like Judy, whose guilt I wrote about in chapter 3, we see the error in our actions or attitudes and must ask forgiveness. Once that has been accomplished we are forgiven by God and the sin is forgotten forever.

However, if we choose to hold on to our guilt, it then crosses over the border into the other, not so easy to get rid of guilt—*false guilt.*

In *Have You Hugged* ... I determined, "False guilt is when we feel burdened and worthless—without scriptural basis. False guilt tears down our self-worth and causes our conscience to nurture our guilts and blow them out of proportion." It is the guilt we make for ourselves, or that which is made for us by our parents, our peers, society, and Satan.

Let's take a look at Karen's case. Karen is fifty-three, divorced, works full-time as a secretary, and lives in a small one-bedroom apartment.

Her father, seventy-eight, requires round-the-clock nursing supervision.

"I didn't know what to do. My brother told me I should bring Dad home to live with me. I couldn't. So I found a suitable nursing home. He seems happy there. But I felt guilty every time I visited. My brother told me it's the cruelest thing I could have done. Some of my friends told me terrible stories about the poor care some relative had gotten in a nursing home. I just became more and more confused and guilty.

"I tried to visit less often but that just compounded my guilt. My decision to place Dad in the home had been a difficult one, but logical. He seemed comfortable and was well cared for, so why the guilt?"

Did Karen suffer from true guilt, or false guilt?

The answer is false guilt. By limiting her visits to the nursing home, Karen did cause some true guilt. The underlying problem, however, was guilt thrown on her shoulders by her brother and some misguided friends.

Karen felt guilty because people told her she'd done a bad thing. Intellectually, she knew she had made the right decision; emotionally, she became trapped in false guilt.

Once she realized why she felt guilty, she could visit her father, see that he was well cared for, and enjoy her time with him without guilt.

In order to solve the guilt problem it is important to differentiate between true and false guilt. If you haven't been able to do that yet here is a chart, created by Dr. DeLoss Friesen for his video series, *Conquering Negative Emotions.* I found it a clear and helpful tool for separating true and false guilt.

Violation of Moral Law

		Yes	No
Feelings	Yes	O.K. (Earned Guilt)	Problem (Learned Guilt)
of			
Guilt	No	Problem	O.K.

In the first box there is an affirmative feeling of guilt and a yes answer to "Violation of Moral Law." That is okay. If you do something wrong, you *should* feel guilty. It's what we call true or *earned guilt.* God forgives our sin and forgets it as soon as we confess and are truly sorry.

In the top box on the right, we feel guilty but have not committed a violation of moral law. If you feel guilty and haven't done anything wrong, you are suffering from false guilt or what Dr. Friesen calls *learned guilt.*

The lower lefthand box tells us that if we have no feelings of guilt and we have violated moral law, we have a big problem. If anyone falls into this category, either the conscience is insensitive to wrong or the person is unaware that a wrong has been done.

Then of course, in the lower right box, if we do not feel guilty and can say, "No, we have not violated the moral law," we're okay. In fact, we would really have cause to celebrate.

So, what do we do when our feelings of guilt are present even when we've done no wrong? First, we acknowledge our innocence. Second, we take steps to stamp out false guilt.

While parenting my teenagers and suffering the load of false guilt, I developed strategies to help me shed the heavy coat of guilt and to better love and care for my kids. The first strategic move is positive thinking, the second, keep laughing, and the third, strive for God's kind of unconditional love.

I believe those strategies work in caring for and loving our aging parents as well. For it is through meeting the needs of others that we lose sight of our own miseries. Besides, the more you care for others, the less reason you have to feel guilty.

"Fix Your Thoughts on What Is True and Good . . ."

There are two kinds of thoughts—negative and positive.

Negative thinkers drag around rumors of ill will, disaster, and impending doom. *Never* and *can't* are the core words in their vocabularies.

Positive thinkers make the best of any situation, accept what can't be changed, and seek solutions to the changeable.

Gary Gorsuch, a positive thinker, has written a delightful book called *Uncle . . . a Jerriatric Love Story.* In the book Gary relates how he and his family made a commitment, out of love, to bring "Uncle" home.

This decision was made in spite of the fact that Gary's wife worked, and they had two teenage daughters. Gary's work involved extensive traveling. They wanted Uncle to live with them, but arranging for his care created a serious problem. Through positive thinking, Gary found a solution. Uncle would travel with him in his job. Unheard of?

As Gary says, "Though a tremendous responsibility and at times a lot of work and inconvenience, caring for Uncle was a privilege which enriched our lives and, I believe, the lives of our family, church and friends." In his book Gary shares what it's like to live with an elderly person. He accepts the bad and dwells on the good.

"A Merry Heart Doeth Good . . ."

Along with positive thinking comes joyfulness. The ability to maintain a sense of humor in whatever circumstances you are in is essential to a long and healthy life. I believe God created laughter as a mechanism to relieve stress, to keep us balanced. Without laughter, stress would wind me up so tight, I'd break. Laughter provides release. When the tension of caring for an aging parent feels like a violin string ready to s-n-a-p-p! loosen up with a belly-jiggling laugh.

Gary and Uncle are an example, not only of positive thinking, but models for maintaining a sense of humor. Throughout his book, Gary relates humorous stories about life with ninety-six-year-old Uncle Charlie.

Uncle had a problem remembering people, even family. He always called Gary Jerry, which was okay. But Uncle's "way with words" often proved embarrassing and very laughable.

> For example, once, after an especially trying day, Uncle was a bit more than confused when we finally got home. Judi met us with a big smile and, for Uncle, a hug and a kiss. He ate it up, savoring every portion of the loving, caring caresses.
>
> After taking full advantage of this attention, Uncle looked up with brimming eyes and said, "Who are you?"
>
> "Why I'm Judi, Gary's wife," she replied.
>
> "Huh, is that so?" snorted Uncle. "Then who in the world are those other women Jerry's with all the time?"

While not everything, and probably not even most things, will be humorous as you care for your aging parents, some will be. So if you can't laugh, try to find the positives.

How can a person maintain a positive attitude and a sense of humor? I only know of one way, through a deep personal relationship with God. Only faith can help us see the light in the middle of a dark and lonely tunnel.

"Beloved, Let Us Love One Another ..."

Berniece Gorsuch, one of Gary's teenage daughters, said it best. "Try to be as patient and understanding as possible. This attitude will be helpful for both parties. Do it out of love rather than grudgingly, doing it as a 'duty.' "

I can't write about love without checking out the Bible's version of what love is: "Love is patient and kind; love is not jealous or boastful; it is not arrogant or rude. Love does not insist on its own way; it is not irritable or resentful; it does not rejoice at wrong, but rejoices in the right. Love bears all things, believes all things, hopes all things, endures all things" (1 Corinthians 13:4–7).

If you're anything like me, that Bible verse arouses a few guilt feelings. Every time I read it I have to admit to my less-than-perfect character. Although in our own strength, we can never achieve this unconditional kind of love, we can hold it up as a goal to work toward.

But even now, there are times when we can know a touch of this perfect love. I have felt it. Have you?

Many times, with my family, or with my patients, I've been on the verge of anger. Then in the middle of my "mad," God inserts the thought, *Love is patient ...* , and I pray. Yes, right there while I'm looking my "enemy" in the eye I say a silent prayer. *Lord, I'm sorry. Help me love this person as You would. Help me see them as You do.*

And if I am open, that perfect love comes. It's like a warm wind suddenly embraces me. My heart is so full of love it spills into my eyes as tears. The feeling is like an emotional whirlwind of compassion, love, peace, empathy, and joy. For a moment I am a loving servant with a God-like heart.

I wish it could stay forever, but it fades away and I'm back to my normal, imperfect self again, doing the best I can.

For me the ability to love the unlovable comes only through God. ". . . if we love one another, God abides in us and his love is perfected in us" (1 John 4:12).

How do we "hang loose" in the face of false guilt? First, we trust in God and His promises to forgive us and sustain us. Second, we ease out negative thoughts and replace them with positives whenever possible. Third, we keep in balance with our ability to laugh. And, fourth, we strive for a true and unconditional love.

Putting away guilt and all the other unwanted negative emotions isn't an instant thing. In fact those feelings will crop up from time to time like thistles in a garden. We must weed them out, pull them up, and fill their space with the best fertilizer available—the positive power of God and prayer.

Now that we've dealt with the emotional side of aging we're ready to move into the more physical areas of help. As our parents grow older they may enter several different phases, from complete independence to requiring total care. In the following chapters we'll discuss topics such as how to prolong their independence, housing options, how and when to help, how and when to choose a nursing home, and how to give physical, emotional, and social care.

5

When the Time Comes

"Honey, I'm really getting worried about Mother," Suzanne remarked. "You should have seen her apartment today. I've never known her to let things go like that."

"Relax, Sue. Mom is doing fine." Ralph placed a reassuring arm around his wife. "Maybe she just had an off day. No need to go getting yourself upset over one little incident."

"This isn't the first time. She doesn't take care of herself anymore. I have to remind her to take baths. Lately, I've been doing her laundry and housework when I visit."

"So, she's getting a bit lazy. At eighty-two, she deserves a break."

"Ralph, it's not that simple," Suzanne frowned. "Remember Mr. Penny, Mother's neighbor?"

Ralph nodded. "Honey, stop pacing. Come sit down and tell me about it."

"Oh, Ralph," Suzanne cried, "she nearly caused a fire yesterday. Mr. Penny told me he smelled smoke and went to check. She put a pan of oatmeal on the stove for her breakfast, then went out to visit a friend and just left it. Mr. Penny said the pan was in flames by the time he got to it."

"Hmmm, why didn't you tell me things were so bad? It's obvious she can't go on living alone."

"I should have seen it sooner," Suzanne admitted. "I just didn't want to think Mother might be anything other than her usual independent self. She's always been active and healthy. . . ."

"Well," Ralph replied, "looks like we can't deny it anymore."

"I know. The apartment manager cornered me today and told me there had been numerous problems with Mother. They'd been taking care of her up until now, but he said she'd have to find some other place to live. He told me they couldn't take any more chances. Ralph," Suzanne leaned against her husband for support, "what are we going to do?"

For Ralph and Suzanne, the time had come. They realized Suzanne's mother could no longer manage her apartment alone.

"What Are We Going to Do?"

The realization that our parents can no longer wave the banner of independence weighs heavy as a suit of armor. And sometimes the responsibility of what to do confines us within those same metal walls.

The best course of action would have been to plan ahead. The best time to plan for old age is when you are young. Yet how many do? If you've chosen to read this book, it may be too late to plan ahead for your aging parents. But, perhaps not.

If your parents are in the early stages of needing your help, or you just think they need help, planning for their future needs may not be an impossibility.

The trouble is that loss of independence for our aging parents often becomes a steel prison for both sides. As with any problem that weighs you down and locks you in, you proceed with caution. Then take steps to solve the problem. Here is a suggested course of action.

Step 1: Evaluate. Should you intervene?
Step 2: Talk it over. The whole family, including the aging parent, if possible, should have some input into this sort of discussion and ultimate decision.
Step 3: List your alternatives.
Step 4: Make a decision and take action.

Evaluate: Do They Really Need Your Help?

Your first step includes knowing when, as well as how, to help. I say *when*, because many adult children place themselves in the "parent" role and feel totally committed to caring for their aging parent even if the older person doesn't need or want help.

Gloria, tells me, "I'm so worried Dad will have an accident, or be mugged. I just hate the thought of him living alone in that house. Since Mom died, I know he isn't eating like he should. But, he refuses to come live with us, or to move into a retirement home. He says he won't leave his garden or his animals."

Many times we worry needlessly about our parents. True, something *could* happen. It's a chance we all take.

I understand completely, however, this idea of worry. I used to panic every time my teenage son would venture out in his car. The anxiety I felt would have been more valid if he'd been walking into an alligator-infested swamp. But alligators or freeways, treacherous mountain crevices or city sidewalks, all invoke worry when we're concerned about the welfare of someone we love.

Just as I paced the floor over my son and his whereabouts, I become anxious about my mother at times. Like when I call and there's no answer. In the back of my mind, I harbor visions of illness or accident— until she comes back from her walk or a trip to the country. Then all is well until the next time.

Sometimes we try to limit the activity of our loved ones because of our fear. Again I am guilty. I have to consider how I would feel if someone tried to stifle me. I'm reminded of this quote from Lewis Carroll's *Alice In Wonderland:*

> "You are old, Father William," the young man said,
> "And your hair has become very white.
> And yet you incessantly stand on your head—
> Do you think, at your age, it is right?"

How often do you box your parents into an "agism" prejudice and say, "You shouldn't be lifting weights at your age," or, "The housework is too much for you, let me do it."

As we observe the capabilities and needs of our parents, we must also evaluate our own feelings and decide whether they really need our help or if we are overreacting.

The other side of the overreaction problem may come from the aging parent who apparently gets along fine, but who continually

comes up with new complaints and worries as a bid for attention.
Many elderly people fall into this category. They are perfectly capable of caring for themselves but, because of fear, need the constant reassurance that someone is available.

Kevin complains, "My father has laid such heavy guilt trips on me I feel like I must weigh 2,000 pounds. He complains when I visit, he complains when I don't. He's afraid to be alone, yet he makes it unbearable for anyone to stay with him."

For the adult child, this behavior in a parent can be very difficult to accept and understand. We fear that perhaps there really is something wrong. What if we chose to ignore the complaint, just this once, and it was real?

As a nurse, I have had my share of difficult patients, and those most hard to handle reacted in much the same way as Kevin's father.

Their fears are very real. Although it's difficult to know why they often continue their complaints in spite of our ministrations and concern, we must continue to care for and encourage them.

I'd like to share a story about a patient whose fears made her demanding and unpleasant, and very hard to love.

Alice lay alone in her hospital room. She had broken her hip. Angry and fearful, she fussed and complained at everyone. I came to work one day to find Alice had been assigned to me. I wanted to call in sick, but it was too late.

Everyone avoided Alice. Who could blame them—the way she screamed at her nurses. I wanted to avoid her too, but when duty calls. . . .

I poked my head in the doorway, took a deep breath, and in my most cheerful tone chirped, "Good morning."

"Didn't sleep well," she mumbled. "Nobody bothered to check on me all night. I could have been dead by this morning. Then you'd have been done with me."

But Alice was very much alive and I wanted to argue against her claims, but only murmured, "Of course we care."

I wondered what caused her anger and deliberate antagonism toward us. *Lord,* I offered a silent prayer, *help me break down this stone barrier of hers. Show me why she's so angry and uncooperative.*

I bathed her and changed the linen on her bed. She raved on, rude and indignant to everything I said. With her care completed, I turned to go. "Can I get you anything, Alice?"

She frowned and said, "It doesn't matter; you'll just forget about it anyway."

I wanted to shout, "That isn't true!" But instead I smiled and promised, "I won't forget you, Alice."

Why does she feel so neglected? I wondered. *She gets more attention than any of the other patients. She's so demanding, yet every time she yells, one of us responds.*

Then it came to me. We seldom stopped in to see her unless she called. Today I would make a point of stopping by her room, even if only to say hello, every half hour or so.

Thank You, Lord, I offered another prayer, *for helping me see, I had to give Alice something from me.* She could demand my time, but until I offered it freely, it wasn't the same.

As the day wore on, my plan of action must have reassured her that I cared. By noon, she'd even given me a smile. Before I left for home that day, I took Alice a rose.

The shine in her tear-filled eyes told me I'd done the right thing.

When I arrived at work the next day they told me Alice had died. A stroke? They weren't sure. The night nurse had made rounds and found her lying there—a rose in her hand, lips curved in a smile.

"Lord," I whispered, "You knew, didn't You?"

Sometimes in trying to help our parents, we look at the physical problems and forget the emotional, social, and spiritual needs. Often, we bypass their fears, intent on our own frustrations and exhaustion caused by their demands.

Should You Intervene? Before you make the arbitrary decision that your parent needs help, evaluate very carefully. Be certain you are not exaggerating or overreacting to their normal aging process.

Perhaps you will need to talk with others such as friends, neighbors, relatives, those who observe your parent in daily activities. These contacts can affirm or negate your suspicions.

Once we put aside our own feelings of fear, and consult others, we can more clearly evaluate our aging parent and decide whether or not intervention is necessary.

At this point, if you feel there must be some kind of change in their present living situation, call a family meeting.

Talk It Over

Discussions involving the future of your aging parent should, of course, include that parent. Naturally, there may be times when your parent cannot participate in the discussion or decision about his or her own care. Most often, however, the aging adult should play an active part.

In this "talking it over" stage, we often must come to grips with yet another problem—*denial.* You can usually expect someone, whether it is the parent, one of your siblings, or some other member of the family, to deny the need for intervention.

This denial complication is just that—complicated. Let's go back to the story at the beginning of this chapter. Sue and Ralph have come to the realization that Sue's mother, Gladys, needs help. They call a family meeting. Sue's brother, Ned, insists, "Mother doesn't need our help. She gets along fine. You're just imagining things. I mean, anyone can make mistakes."

Gladys also insists all is well and echoes Ned's sentiments. "I won't move and they can't make me. I don't forget things. Mr. Penny doesn't like me, never has. How can you believe all those lies about me?"

Sue and Ralph have hit headlong into the stone hedge called denial. Ned cannot accept the fact that his mother, the always present and controlling adult factor in his life, could be unstable. Parents aren't supposed to need their kids. It is all a part of the inability to accept our human mortality.

Gladys denies, in part because she doesn't want to admit she has a problem, and in part because she forgets she has forgotten.

What should Sue and Ralph do? First of all they can wait until an accident or traumatic event mows through the hedge and forces Ned to see the problem. Second, they can take charge and find a place where Gladys can receive the special care she needs, but then they risk alienating the family.

What would you do? Sue and Ralph know Gladys needs their assistance. So, with or without Ned's cooperation, they explore alternatives to find the best care for her. They decide to bring Gladys to their home for a trial period. With little coaxing, she agrees. So, to their surprise, does Ned. Could it be that part of Ned's denial included a fear that he would have to accept the responsibility for her care?

Talking it over isn't easy. Sometimes the discussions turn to fiery arguments, or explode in all-out war between family members. But, when talking doesn't work, you simply do what you can and pray for solutions.

List Your Alternatives

When the time comes and your parent needs help, whether it is in the form of a few physical changes in his or her environment, or full-time nursing care, the steps for helping are the same: Make a fair, thoughtful, and prayerful evaluation, talk it over, then, list the alternatives.

In the next chapter we'll explore the various housing options available to the elderly. For now, I'll suggest a plan of attack to find available services in your area and to determine what is best for you and your aging parent.

For starters, do a financial analysis of your parents' income and properties to determine what monies are available. Knowing their financial situation is a must before you look into various housing options, health care, and government assistance programs.

Next, take a walk through the Yellow Pages of your phone directory. If you look under Aging, you'll probably find a list of "see also's." In mine I see, Home Health Services, Family Counselors, Retirement Communities & Homes, Senior Citizens' Service, Social Service Organizations, and Social Workers.

How do we know where to call? Good question. Sometimes it's nearly impossible to manipulate your way through the bureaucratic maze.

I recently spoke with a representative for the Southwest Washington Agency on Aging. By following a series of leads I managed to break the governmental code and find the agency designed to assist you and your aging parent.

Mr. George Telisman, the director, advised me that there is a national network of services for the elderly, but admitted they are hard to find. I agree. Even after talking with him, I went back to my phone book at home and still had trouble finding the agency he had told me about.

Mr. Telisman said, "The best place to start is with the Senior Citizen Information and Assistance Referral Agency. This agency is available in every community. It is funded to help steer people in the right direction. They can also help you to assess the situation and let you know about all the services available in the community."

One of the problems is *the name of this agency varies from county to county*. In Clark County, Washington, it is listed in the telephone book on the first page under COMMUNITY SERVICES NUMBERS under the subheading, Aging, as *Senior Assistance/Case Management*. The key words to look for as your check your telephone book under county or city listings are *senior, aging, information, assistance,* and *case management*.

Who would have thought it? I, for one, would never have thought of looking there.

If you still can't locate this helpful government agency write for information on services for the aging in your community. Send your query to: National Association of Area Agencies on Aging, Suite 208, 600 SW Maryland Avenue, Washington, D.C. 20024.

The basic purpose of these government agencies designed to help the elderly is to develop a continuum of support and care. Services provide assistance to the vulnerable elderly (the poor, sickly)—those in danger of being institutionalized. The goal here is to keep them in the community and out of nursing homes for as long as possible.

There is a recent emphasis on helping us. (Yes, us—the care-givers.) According to the director of the SW Washington Agency on Aging, "80 percent of the elderly are cared for by an informal support system. That is, they are supported by friends and relatives. There is a growing trend to recognize this 80 percent by the government.

"We feel," Mr. Telisman continued, "that if we offer help to the family care-givers, the home care will continue longer. We offer help so they don't burn out. It costs less to provide some home care and other services occasionally to help out the family than to pay the cost of nursing home or institutionalized care."

This assistance program provided by the government is not to be considered welfare, but rather a helping hand. Charges for services usually correspond with ability to pay.

As I continued my explorations and research, I ran across an organization called *Staff Builders Health Care Services.* Staff Builders offers total home health care, "from skilled nursing care and therapists to home health aides and companions—by the hour, for visits, or 24 hours a day if needed."

In addition, I found when I interviewed at a Staff Builders office, that they offer themselves as a resource to the community. In other words, if you need help but don't know which way to turn, they will provide counsel and assist you in finding the right alternatives.

They tell me they even have the ability to steer you to government agencies that will best meet your needs. Now that's a plus.

Staff Builders has offices in major cities all over the United States and in Toronto, Canada. Check the white pages of the telephone directory or, for more information, write: Executive Director, Staff Builders Home Health Care, Inc., Dept. M, 122 East 42nd Street, New York, N.Y. 10168.

As you continue to gather information that will help you decide how you can best help your aging parent, check the telephone directory under Retirement Communities & Homes. The listing here will give you an idea of the housing available to the elderly. You will want to visit several. Actually, that may be the last thing you want to do, but do it anyway. It's good for you. And besides, you need to know what's out there.

At this point, I'd suggest you put together a three-by-five-inch card file, one card for each place you visit. Write the following information on each card:

NAME_____
Address_____ Phone _____
Type: (Example: Retirement apartment)
Qualifications: (Example: Independent Living/Skilled Nursing Care)
Impression: (Clean, residents seemed well cared for, etc.)
Costs: (Be specific and all inclusive.)

File these cards under the appropriate heading, Retirement Homes, Nursing Homes, and so on.

In addition to looking for available homes, check out the listings under Home Health Services and Nurses and Nursing Homes. Make up cards for each of the services interviewed and the costs, including those government assistance programs we talked about.

Does that sound like a lot of work? It is. But you need to explore on your own to find out what is available. Perhaps right now all your parent requires is an occasional ride to a doctor's office, or possibly home-delivered meals, day care, or shopping assistance. But while you're gathering information it doesn't hurt to store it so that if and when you need more help, you'll know where to go and who to contact.

Primarily, your alternatives will include: retirement homes—independent and semi-independent living; shared housing; foster homes for adults; home health care (in varying degrees); adult day care facilities; respite care; community resources (meals, transportation, etc.); convalescent centers; and nursing homes.

Taking Action

Once you've found what is available in your community, talk through the choices. Decisions may be difficult; mostly because no one can make them for you. Once you've determined how much help your parent requires, and know what resources to choose from, it's time to take action.

That may sound like a simple step, but actually, making the decision may be easier than moving ahead with your choice.

Your decision may require a remodeling job of your parent's present home, or perhaps moving him or her into a new apartment or into your home. Whatever the decision there will be some major adjustments for everyone involved.

The following chapters will offer help and guidance in choosing a home, maintaining independence, dealing with and recognizing medical problems, developing necessary skills for home care and nursing home care, and financial matters.

When the time comes, when the aging parent or an elderly person in your life needs help, some preliminary homework will give you an edge. Perhaps the time has already come. Whichever the case, read on and get yourself generously supplied with help and hope so you can cope—when the time comes.

6

Where Will They Live?

There are more housing options available for the elderly today than ever before. And it's a good thing. There are more elderly comprising our population than ever before.

From Baby Boom to Aging Boom

The United States Census Bureau projects that by the year 2030, one in every five Americans will be sixty-five or older. Currently every one in ten, about 27.4 million people, fall into the sixty-five-plus category. That means by 2030 most of us will be part of the 64.3 million elderly.

By my calculations I will be eighty-seven that year. Gray Panthers, here I come! While we are now in the process of seeking out housing options for our parents, let's put some thought into our own futures as well. Lobbying for legislative changes now may not only help our parents but us too.

Living Alone and Loving It

Most of us cringe at the thought of our kids having to take care of us in our senior years. And although we may see caring for an aging parent as not only a responsibility, but as something we want to do, they may not be any more willing to accept our help than we would want to accept aid from our kids.

For most people, maintaining independence is a priority goal. In a recent newspaper article, David Ammons of the Associated Press stated, "Maintaining their health and staying in their own homes becomes an all-important passion for older people. Poverty, devastating illness, and the nursing home loom as dreaded specters."

Keeping the elderly independent as long as possible, as I wrote in the last chapter, is the goal of government agencies and should be our goal as well. But getting through the bureaucracy to find out how can be tough. Still, I encourage you to work with your parents to take advantage of the services offered in your community.

Remember back in chapter 2 where I said that only 5 percent of the elderly will require institutional type care? That means most senior citizens will not end up in a nursing home.

In fact, many of our parents will conclude their days living alone and loving it with very little or no help from us. While some will want to stay in the home you grew up in, many will opt for a more mobile way of life.

The Migratory "Snowbirds"

Just because a spouse dies, or retirement arrives doesn't mean your parent will move out of his or her home. But many do. In fact, often at retirement we find seniors packing it in, pulling up roots, and heading for "greener (or sunnier) pastures." There has been a trend among older Americans in the last few years to retire to the sunbelt regions, or to special vacation spots where they always wanted to settle.

A few years ago Aunt Olga and Uncle Wes donned retirement feathers and became "snowbirds" as they sold their home, bought a large motor home, and migrated South for the winter—Yuma to be exact. They loved their newfound freedom. Even after Uncle Wes died, Olga still makes her way South in the fall. They sold their home and moved to a less confining life-style because they wanted to.

Staying Home

On the other hand, many seniors want to stay home. They are not so willing to pull up their roots. Sally's eighty-three-year-old father,

Jack, *will not* move from the farm he's nurtured for fifty years. Since his wife, Marta, died Sally worries about Jack living alone. Her primary concerns are that he doesn't eat properly or that he might have an accident.

Sally insists he move into the city where she can watch him. Jack refuses. He is comfortable and secure in the familiar surroundings of his rural home. Should Jack have to move so that he can receive the attention he needs?

Sally thought so until she investigated some of the alternatives that could keep Jack independent and in his home. With the help of friends, neighbors, and a home health aide, Jack manages to maintain his independence.

Maybe you're thinking, *If Jack needs that much help, how can you say he's living independently?*

Good question. Actually, total independence is a myth. Very few people ever function completely independently of others. More simply, independent living is being able to stay in one's own home or apartment with or without adjustments, plus a few helpful hands.

For the most part, many elderly like Jack can get along. They just need someone to mow the lawn, perhaps assist with housework, do the heavy maintenance work, and look in on them every now and then.

Staying in their home can be a financial help as well as giving emotional security. The home may have low payments or be entirely paid for.

Having Your Home and Selling It Too

In addition to the above solutions, there is the possibility of converting home equity into retirement income. This is a fairly new concept and is still in its experimental stages.

Essentially, the program involves allowing an elderly person to sell the house while continuing to live in it. There are various options in this concept. For example, an investor might buy the house and make a down payment and monthly payments, then lease it back to the previous owner for monthly payments. Confusing? Let's try an example.

Suppose you were to buy your elderly parent's home. You would make a down payment and monthly payments. The house is yours. Now instead of moving in yourself, you rent it out to your parent. The parent has the financial gain of the sale, yet can continue to live in the house, possibly for life.

Quite simply the elderly can convert their most valuable asset, home equity, into cash. Their locked-up assets convert to liquid assets to be used now when they need them, and at the same time they can remain in their home.

For more information on this interesting and perhaps financially rewarding concept write to: National Center for Home Equity Conversion, 110 East Main, Room 1010, Madison, Wis. 53703.

Then again many seniors would rather sell out and move into a home with less upkeep such as an apartment or mobile home.

Mobile Homes

My husband's father and stepmother, for example, recently sold their triplex and bought a mobile home in a retirement mobile home community. The community offers many social events and privacy, and little upkeep of the home and grounds.

Although they discussed the move with us, it was their decision and their plan for the future.

My mother similarly found herself with a rural home when Dad died. After talking over the possibilities, she decided to sell the house and purchase a mobile home, in a small rural community. She maintains a bit of country while at the same time is able to walk into town to shop and commune with neighbors.

Another excellent benefit for our parents was that the money they made by selling their homes and moving into less expensive quarters brings in good-sized supplements to their monthly incomes. This may be a possibility for your parents as well. Social Security checks need all the supplementing they can get.

Besides mobile homes, we see an abundance of retirement homes and communities being built to meet the specific needs of the independent aging.

Retirement Havens

Retirement complexes and communities abound, yet many have waiting lists. For reasonable rates (some are government subsidized), an older person may rent or buy an apartment or condominium that offers all the comforts—pleasant surroundings, companionship, crafts, classes, outings, food, and fun.

One such retirement community in my area currently offers apartments from $463 per month for a studio to $1,009 for a two bedroom/two bath. Meals can be purchased for an additional fee with a choice of one, two, or three meals a day. Residents, however, must be ambulatory—that is able to walk to meals and to pick up mail every day.

The retirement counselor there stated, "Because of the required ambulation, activities, and companionship, some of our residents' health actually improves after they move here."

There are many such housing facilities available for the elderly. Developer Tom MacDonald of Portland, Oregon, has recently begun building complexes such as this in Oregon and California. There is a great need for more of these homes for the elderly population. Tom has researched extensively and builds retirement complexes to meet the special needs of older people. He makes certain his complexes are affordable and comfortable.

I might add a word of caution here. Some retirement homes can be very expensive; but for many, such as Tom's, government subsidy is available. You and your parent(s) should check the costs and benefits thoroughly before making a decision. For information on such housing call (503) 222-4500 in Oregon or (415) 935-1660 for the San Francisco area.

Shared Housing

Another option for the elderly who hold tight to their independence yet could use a little help from their friends, is shared housing. While live-in help runs about seventy-five dollars a day plus room and board, shared housing could bring in a rental income, or simply provide an exchange of services.

For example, seventy-eight-year-old Helen has a three-bedroom home. Helen wants to share her home with a college student in exchange for companionship and doing odd jobs she can't handle herself.

More and more people share the responsibility of a home these days to cut expenses. Why not the elderly? Of course, shared housing is not without its problems. However, there are organizations such as the Shared Housing Resource Center, Inc., 6344 Greene Street, Philadelphia, Pa. 19144, a nonprofit agency that can provide you with further information on the concept, plus a national directory of shared housing programs.

The idea of these independent living programs is to keep the elderly parent out of a nursing home and in the community for as long as possible. However, eventually we will probably have to consider options for the semi-independent, those who no longer can live independently without daily supervision or assistance.

Semi-Independent Living Harder to Find

Housing for those senior citizens who need regular medical supervision, or general assistance, yet can function in part on their own, is not as easily found.

Many of the retirement homes I wrote about earlier do allow for some minor disabilities and provide some medical assistance. In fact, if you can utilize some of the government assistance programs—such as partial home health, grocery shopping, meals on wheels—plus your own input, the aging parent may be able to stay in this environment indefinitely.

Some retirement homes offer a continuing care program. In addition to offering retirement home benefits to the independent senior citizen, a contract assures shelter and services for the rest of that person's life.

For an entry fee (or endowment) of from $10,000 to $100,000 plus monthly care fees of $200 to $2,500 a retiree can be guaranteed lifetime care. Benefits usually include an apartment, one to three meals a day, utilities, building maintenance, activities, health care, and eventually, if necessary, complete nursing care. Services vary.

For the person who actually ends up needing extensive medical care for many years, the program would provide that care. However, people who will never need nursing home care may end up paying a great deal for the additional "insurance."

I would caution you and your aging parent to weigh the cost carefully and consider the options. Also, you'll need to do a careful screening on this type of service. Although many are reputable and give good care to the end, some have been known to give poor and even abusive treatment to those needing extensive care, especially when the money runs out.

And there are many additional options such as sheltered housing, group homes, foster homes for adults, your home, and of course, nursing homes.

Sheltered Housing

Sheltered housing is similar to home sharing, yet the tenants of a sheltered home generally suffer a greater degree of disability. They may be permanently or temporarily, physically or mentally impaired. In a sheltered home, the individuals have the protection of community as well as a "house person" to look after them.

Group homes provide a similar service—a sheltered environment, along with services specified by the individual's need designed to keep the elderly as independent as possible.

Foster Homes

Just as the government provides foster homes for displaced children, foster homes are available for the elderly. In my community, foster homes are supported by the Department of Social and Health Services. These facilities are also designed to keep the elderly out of the nursing home and in the community as long as possible.

The foster home provides shelter, meals, and a feeling of "family." This is an especially positive alternative for you if your aging parent lives in another state. The foster family can provide your parent with a loving home environment.

Also, the concept is one you may want to consider in an effort to help the elderly in your community.

Bringing Parents Into Your Home

More and more adult children dutifully bring their aging parent into their homes with the intent of providing the best possible care and companionship. Many make the decision out of love and a desire to serve, some decide out of a sense of responsibility, while yet others bring their parents home because financial limitations leave them with no other choice.

Bringing a parent home has many positive qualities. Togetherness as a family unit provides a loving and caring environment for the aging parent. Children benefit from the wisdom of old age, also from the ability to see and understand the life process. Live-in grandparents offer a special kind of relationship to children—someone to love them no matter what and to spoil them a little.

A grandparent can share family roots, history, and faith and can impart wisdom to a questioning child. Grandparents who are still able to function in part can bake cookies, teach crafts such as sewing or woodwork, or tell stories.

Besides, there's a certain amount of satisfaction in caring for someone who really needs you.

Yet, if the relationship between you and your parent has always been tense or stormy, don't expect it to change now. Just because you fantasize yourself as a loyal, loving child don't think your fantasy can't turn into a nightmare. A quote in a recent *Los Angeles Times* article by Herman Wong states, "There's nothing romantic or idealistic about this. If a parent and child have never been close and loving, that's not going to change now. You have to be realistic and honest."

Please don't misunderstand me. I strongly encourage adult children to open their homes to their aging parents. Just think it through carefully before you do. Know ahead of time what will be required of you. Communicate with your family. Are they willing? Don't give up a good relationship with your spouse to accommodate a parent.

If you and your family do decide your home is the best place for Mom or Dad, here are some suggestions to make the transition easier.

Often, having a parent live in an attached apartment or nearby mobile home or other living quarters rather than sharing the same house creates a better environment for everyone. For some, the live-in arrangement works well. But even in the most peaceful of families, conflicts will arise.

Anticipate the problems before they come and resolve them before, not after, the move. If your parent needs nursing care, read chapter 10 on nursing skills you should acquire. Learn what support groups are available in your area for people who care for their parents. Also, familiarize yourself with community services such as Adult Day Care Centers, Home Health Care Services—the kind of help that provides relief for you.

I mentioned in the last chapter that the government agencies on aging are trying to give more help to people who care for their parents at home. One of the services that is becoming more widely available is "respite care." It simply means that the family care-givers will be able to take planned or emergency time off while a trained volunteer provides the care.

Even though difficulties arise it is possible to compromise, accept the situation, and make the best of it. For all the problems, all the faults, there really is "no place like home."

Now suppose you get all the kinks worked out? You want to bring your aging parent home and everybody agrees. Great. Set aside your own dreams for the moment and develop a servant's heart. Prepare yourself to give. Give compassion, love, and the care that only you, a loving and caring child, can offer to the parent who needs you. Give, for as long as you can. And if or when the time comes and you're all given out, consider the next alternative.

Nursing Homes

Possibly, you will never have to consider nursing home care. You may cringe to even think about a nursing home for your parent. However, if that parent comes to a point where he or she requires more than you can give, for both your sakes, you may need to consider it.

Unless:

- You are willing and physically able to work twenty-four hours a day.
- You are able to get relief from other family members, respite care, or a home health aide or nurse.
- You have the nursing skills required to care for and cope with the geriatric patient.
- You can remain joyful and supportive, providing not only physical care, but social, emotional, and spiritual care as well.

Nursing homes, contrary to much popular belief, are not dungeons. And, it is not a sin to place your elderly parent in one. The sin begins when an elderly parent is "dumped" into an institution and forgotten.

Many nursing homes provide excellent round-the-clock geriatric care. Some currently have specialized Alzheimer's units, where doctors and nurses have the most up-to-date treatment and methods of care at their disposal.

Geriatric nurses specialize in caring for elderly patients. Most of them do so because they love the elderly and want to see them well cared for. There is a Geriatric Nurses Association in the United States with chapters in nearly every community. The nurses who belong are committed to making certain their elderly patients get the best possible care. These nurses work as home health nurses, in hospitals, and in nursing or convalescent homes.

I'd encourage you not to be afraid of putting your elderly parent in their capable care. Certainly, not all nursing homes are high quality. In fact, some really are dumps.

Several years ago a federal crackdown on nursing homes forced most of them to either close down or come up to government standards. You must choose a nursing home with the same care you would use in choosing a residence for yourself. You will find out how to choose a nursing home and how to care for your aging parent in a nursing home in chapter 11.

We've gone through the many alternatives to the question, "Where will they live?"

Now, let's back up to the independent life. Often, by making a few changes in the elderly parent's home—perhaps some remodeling or creating a safer environment—your aging parent may be able to stay in that independent life-style for an indefinite period. The next chapter talks about alterations—some simple, some more complex—and services that can provide a happier and healthier home environment for your aging parent.

7

Maintaining Independence: How You Can Help

A Place of My Own
I like tidying up this place, Lord,
Sweeping up, wiping the sink,
Making the faucets shine.
It's not all that grand of a place, Lord,
But thank the Lord, Lord, it's mine.
It upsets my children to see me here.
"You don't have to live like this, Pop.
Live with one of us," they say.
"There's room. We'd love to have you."
What can I say?
I sound stubborn, ungrateful,
But I don't want to leave this place.
I'm lonely, sure. But there's nothing they can do
    about that.
Now that Margaret's gone and they're all grown,
Having a place of my own,
Snug as a ship's cabin, helps.
It's comforting. And You'll be here with me, Lord,
If, as they keep saying, "something happens."
What do they mean "if"? When.

ELISE MACLAY
Green Winter

Like this man, most older people cherish their independence. Yet, a slip on December ice may result in a fractured hip, a stroke could

67

cause partial paralysis, arthritis can cause crippling disabilities—and steal their freedom. Too many times the disabled elderly are refused the chance to make it on their own. They are moved into a place where they can be taken care of instead of learning to live with their handicaps.

Before you rush to find a retirement complex, check your parent into a nursing home, or bring your parent home, ask yourself this question: *What can I do to adjust their present living quarters so they don't have to move?*

Little Things Mean a Lot

Growing old, as we saw in chapter 2 on aging awareness, may bring along with it diminishing use of arms and legs, diminishing eyesight, hearing loss, speech impairment, loss of senses such as taste, smell, and touch.

Any of these sensory changes can have emotional and psychological effects such as fear, paranoia, depression, irritability, and confusion. Often the elderly have been misdiagnosed as having Alzheimer's or some other form of senile dementia only to have the problem traced back to one or more of these losses.

In addition loss of body function is often the contributing cause of accidents among the elderly.

These sensory changes could determine whether or not a person can remain independent. By modifying their environment you can help them cope, and provide a safe and supportive living situation.

Let's have a look at each in turn and see how you can help.

Put Yourself in a Wheelchair

Often the elderly, because of illness, weakness, or debilitating accidents, must use a mechanical device in order to get around. Canes, walkers, and wheelchairs are the most commonly used.

In order for your parent to remain independent and still use any of these helpful devices, the home he or she lives in may need a remodeling job.

One of the best ways to determine what changes, if any, need to be made, is to put yourself in the elderly person's place. Walk around the house with a walker, or try managing in a wheelchair.

1. Are the front steps too narrow? Should you replace them with a ramp? Go ahead, try running your set of wheels up the stairs. Even in a walker, the stairs may be too narrow for safety.
2. Are there any area rugs to slip on?
3. Any door sills to trip over?
4. Are the door spaces wide enough? You say you zipped through the door and smashed your hand between the wheel and the door?
5. Are closets and cupboards easily accessible?
6. What tasks will be impossible for the disabled person to do?
7. Who will take over the responsibility of those tasks?
8. Have safety grips been built in the bathroom for easy access into the tub, shower, and onto the toilet? Tub and shower should have nonskid surfaces to prevent slipping.
   Come on, give it a try. Wheel yourself up to the toilet, grab the bar (remember, you can't use your legs), and swing yourself up and . . . Oops! You say you overshot the pot? It's okay, you'll get better with age.
9. Stairs may have to be avoided entirely, but if used be certain handrails are placed on both sides and stairs are free of clutter.

As you maneuver your way through the house, you'll get an idea of the necessary changes that will make independent living easier for your parent. Make a list. Calculate the expense, the feasibility. Can the changes be made or will it be necessary to move into a different, safer environment?

Other problems can come with arthritis. Sometimes just getting dressed in the morning can be as frustrating as pushing a 2-inch button into a ¾-inch hole. Speaking of getting dressed, there are businesses specializing in clothing for the handicapped. I know of a woman in Eugene, Oregon, who does just that. Check through your local organizations that offer help to the handicapped and the elderly and see chapter 14 for more information on this.

More ideas that can make life easier for and help the elderly and handicapped function can be found in a book called *An Easier Way* by Jean Vieth Sargent. The book contains over two hundred hints with illustrations which "can be achieved with minimum expense and effort. Help is offered for every kind of disability."

Some of the gadgets included are a sock "taker-offer," writing aids for the arthritic, a key holder for weak hands, cups for shaky hands, a wheelchair patient's door opener and closer, a non-stooping foot mop, and an expandable-eye needle for easy threading.

Another helpful book in this area is called the *Catalog of Aids for the Disabled*, by Nancy and Jack Kreisler.

Through the Looking Glass Dimly

Although prescription lenses often correct vision loss, not all visual changes respond to treatment. For example, many older people experience problems with glare and depth perception. They may find it difficult to distinguish colors. Because of this, stairs, curbs, and uneven walking surfaces can be potential hazards.

Recently I went to an exhibit on aging at the Oregon Museum of Science and Industry. As a part of the exhibit we were encouraged to wear special glasses that simulated this visual problem. As I walked into a make-believe kitchen with my "old" eyes, the first thing I noticed was how all the dull, soft shades of color blended together. It was practically impossible to distinguish containers. A can of oven cleaner looked just like a can of Pam cooking spray through my lenses. The gray of a sidewalk curb, its shadow, and the street blended, making the entire area look flat. Have you ever stepped off a curb you didn't know was there? Scary and dangerous. How much more dangerous for the elderly than for us.

You can never quite imagine what it is like to look through dim windows until you've done it. Try to imagine a world through your elderly parent's eyes, then make the changes in their world that can help them see better.

1. Mark railings, curbs, corners, and steps with a bright color tape.
2. Reduce glare with diffused lighting, sheer curtains to shut out bright sunlight; use textured rather than smooth reflective surfaces.
3. Use more warm, bright, contrasting colors. Reds, oranges, and yellows are easier to see than cool colors.
4. Get books with large print and use large print for marking labels and telephone numbers (get a large number insert for the tele-

phone face), and create your own directory with emergency and most used numbers.

5. Since drugs can be one of the worst problems for the elderly, make certain they are necessary and clearly labeled, and that the directions are written in large bold letters. Check with your parent occasionally to be certain he or she is able to read the labels and follow the directions.

6. Keep knives and sharp objects in a special place. Remove all unnecessary sharp objects.

7. Walk around the house with your parent and ask him or her to tell you if there is an area where glare is a problem.

8. Keep house free of clutter. After children come to visit, be certain all toys are put away.

Hearing Loss

Hearing diminishes in about a third of the people over sixty. If you suspect your aging parent has a hearing problem, encourage him or her to face the problem and get the devices that can help improve hearing.

Even with the use of a hearing aid, sounds are not always clear. A hearing aid amplifies all sounds and is not like normal good hearing. It is difficult for a person wearing a hearing aid to understand rapid speech so you will need to slow down when you talk. Also, face the person, get his or her attention. Background noises such as music, lawn mowers, crowd noises are often confusing and more audible than a person speaking close by.

A person with a hearing problem may experience emotional problems such as paranoia, suspicion, isolation. Have you ever missed the punch line of a joke or an important phrase in a conversation? Remember how left out you felt when everyone else was laughing or responding? Did you compensate? Did you feel the joke was on you? Did you feel frustrated? Sad? Magnify those feelings a hundred or more times a day. See what I mean?

You can help your aging parent overcome a hearing problem. Here's how:

1. If you suspect hearing loss, encourage your parent to have an exam. Many people, especially women, tend to compensate and

have a hard time admitting to sensory losses. Also, be certain that the hearing loss really is a permanent physical impairment. Some elderly people may develop a buildup of earwax, which can cause hearing loss. The wax is easily removed. The result? Instant hearing.

2. Give them a little assertiveness training. There's no need to feel embarrassed or ashamed of a hearing loss. Encourage them to let people know they don't hear well.

3. Educate others and yourself to better communicate with those suffering hearing loss.

- Advise the hearing loss victim of changes in conversation.
- Speak more slowly.
- Use lower moderate tones—*not louder.*
- Enunciate clearly.
- Face the listener.
- Catch the attention of the person before speaking.
- Provide adequate lighting.
- Reduce background noises.

4. Purchase an amplifier for the telephone and a flashing light that signals the telephone is ringing. Earphones for the television and/or radio may be helpful. Bear in mind that when the ears are full of radio or television, the doorbell may not be hearable. One possibility would be to train a dog to bark, run around in circles, and generally make a complete nuisance of himself when the doorbell or phone rings.

Hearing is important to us. Imagine echoes of clanging cymbals; the low groans of a grinding wheel. Imagine silence. Imagine helping someone hear again.

Speech Impairment

Millie Walters, seventy-two, has had a stroke. She can't talk. Her entire right side is paralyzed. Her eyes communicate fear, frustration, yearning. Her mouth moves, sounds break through, jumbled sounds, the kind a babe might make. But there are no coos, no smiles, only tears.

Communication has become an impassible barrier. How can we help her and others like her break down the barrier and feel a part of the world again?

1. Ask simple questions that require a yes or no answer.
2. Provide a tablet at all times for writing notes.
3. Communicate through silent messages, hugs, smiles, eyes that say, "I love you." Touch surpasses language barriers.
4. Reflect back that you understand the frustration, the anger, and pain. The greatest communication two people can share is to understand each other.
5. Reassure her with your patience and your presence. So often people with a handicap or sensory loss are neglected in the communicating world. Whether from fear, embarrassment, or just lack of empathy and time, the victim is passed over quickly and even shunned.

Loss of Taste, Smell, Touch . . .

What harm can a loss of taste, smell, or touch do? Plenty.

Loss of taste brings a loss of appetite. Poor nutrition may follow. Include the loss of smell and the problem compounds.

Safety becomes a factor when you consider our sense of smell can warn of smoke, spoiled food, gas leaks, and so on. In addition, not being able to smell may result in poor hygiene.

Sensory loss of touch means a decreased sensitivity to pain. A person with loss of feeling on his or her skin surface may suffer burns and minor irritations and not be aware of it. Stove burns present the biggest safety problem. Because of the decreased sensitivity to pain, doctors may have difficulty locating a problem area. This is especially true with a confused person. Consequently, if the elderly patient becomes irritable, it's a good idea to check for a pain problem first.

"Am I Losing My Mind?"

Sensory losses may bring about confusion. The victim may wonder, *Am I losing my mind?* Being deprived of the normal senses may cause the following problems.

1. Lack of attention to detail
2. Inability to receive information clearly
3. Overstimulation which results in "tuning out" and a decrease in attentiveness
4. Inhibited learning ability—poor attention span
5. Increased stress
6. Inappropriate emotional reactions
7. Submissiveness and/or dependency
8. Hallucinations
9. Inappropriate sexual behavior
10. A misdiagnosis of "senile dementia"

You can see how something we may label a "minor problem" could balloon into a major explosion of symptoms. Awareness on your part can help alleviate the confusion.

Afraid to Leave Your Parent Alone?

Fear that a parent may have an accident or need someone to respond to a medical emergency may have you wondering if they really should live alone.

There are several communication systems available that can lay your worry to rest.

One is LIFELINE, a Personal Emergency Response Program, provided through Lifeline Systems, Inc., Waltham, Mass. LIFELINE operates through a local hospital. It works like this:

1. Your parent carries a small, wireless help button in a pocket or attached to clothing. Any time he or she needs help they simply push the button to contact the hospital's emergency response center.
2. This "help" call activates a unit that is attached to the home telephone. It automatically dials the hospital. LIFELINE says the "home unit can work even if your phone is off the hook and during power failure."
3. When the call comes in, trained coordinators at the hospital emergency response center will:

- Immediately try to reach your parent by telephone to see what help he or she needs.
- If unable to contact your parent, send a "responder" to the home.
- These "responders" are people you have selected in advance (you, a friend, relative, neighbor, or anyone else you choose to be called in the event of an emergency).

4. Upon arrival at your parent's home, the responder resets the LIFELINE unit. This signals the hospital to call your parent's home and the responder can then tell the hospital what kind of help is needed.
5. There is yet another feature to the LIFELINE unit which allows the unit to automatically signal the hospital if the timer has not been reset. (The timer is reset each time the telephone is used.)

Staff Builders offers a similar but more advanced program called Communicare. Communicare establishes a two-way voice communication with a Staff Builder's home station thereby continuously giving reassurance to the client until help arrives. It also helps the client verbalize the problem so proper help can be dispatched. It may be some problem other than medical, such as fire, break-in, or just a lonely person needing the comfort and friendliness of a caring voice. For information ask for the Communicare brochure, from your local Staff Builders office or write to: Staff Builders Health Care Services, 122 East 42nd Street, New York, N.Y. 10168.

In addition there may be volunteer "Telephone Reassurance" chapters in your area. These operate under the headings Telecare, Caring, or Ring-a-day. Volunteers make daily phone calls at a prearranged time to the elderly and disabled. If after several calls within an hour the caller receives no answer, someone visits the home and medical assistance is summoned if necessary.

Information about the program can be obtained from the AARP (American Association of Retired Persons) Catalog of Publications and Materials.

We've dealt with many physical needs in which a little help can lengthen your parents' independence time. Now I'd like to address the mental and emotional areas and the need for social stimulation, which can have just as much influence on the well-being of your parent.

A Need to Be Needed

One of the greatest dangers among the elderly population is retirement. To many, retirement from their jobs means, "You are no longer needed by society."

I spoke to a woman recently who confessed, "I taught school for forty-three years and people always treated me with respect. When I retired it was like I suddenly became senile. I lost my identity. No one thinks of me as a teacher anymore, just an old woman. Just because I no longer teach in a school I can still be useful to someone, can't I?"

The retirement syndrome along with our youth-oriented culture have contributed to a serious problem for the aged today—age discrimination.

Somewhere we got the idea being old equaled being useless and unnecessary. Perhaps the saddest part is that so many elderly people really believe it. For years "old" has been a very unpopular thing to be.

Fortunately, attitudes toward aging are picking up. George Burns claims to be "making old age popular." As he said in one of his interviews, "I can't die, I'm booked to do a show in Las Vegas in ten years."

Today aging Americans have many heroes. Television commercials now use older people to sell products. Some of these ads have become successful overnight. Making the most of your aging has become the topic of many books.

One of those is Charlotte Hale's book *The Super Years.* She tells people to make the most of their senior years, offers a cure to common loneliness, tells how to create new energy and develop new careers and hobbies, and how to improve health. "Age means little when you're in love with life," says Charlotte. Maybe reading this book or one like it can boost the morale of your aging parent.

Psychology Today, January 1984, ran a section on "Aging Americans." One article, "The Art of Aging," had photographs and quotes from several octogenarians. One of those, Otto Luening, eighty-five, an accomplished musician says, "Tuning people out at 65, 70, or 85 is a social waste. If people have a given capacity and it grows with age, there should be a way for them to use it."

Another, Raphael Soyer, painter, says, "I face new challenges every day. I want to do larger, more complex compositions that will test my new skills and will be difficult to fulfill. Every painting I do is just as if I've never painted before. I am now 84 years old, and when people ask me, 'Are you still painting?' it's like being asked, 'Are you still breathing?' "

Optimism. Positive thinking. This is the source of vitality and a love of life, no matter what the actual age. And while there are many who can say, "I love being my age; I love growing older; I'm living my life to the fullest"; there are many more who say, "I'm too old. There's no reason for me to live. No one needs me. I'm just a burden to you."

If your aging parent is one of those who feel useless, depressed, and "old," let's look at some more ways to lift them out of the pits and into a joyful life.

I talked earlier about being needed. Everyone wants to feel someone or something needs them. Therapy may in some cases be as simple as providing the older person with plants and animals. Plants can be great therapy. Getting one's hands into dirt, pulling weeds, nurturing the soil, and watching growth can reduce stress, relieve anxieties, and take the mind off present problems.

An animal can provide an elderly person with more than just a chore; it is a warm friend who depends on them for food and shelter. I just saw a special on cats the other night on television. There is a home in Portland that houses 100 cats and varying numbers of confused, messed-up teenagers. The cats are there to be loved, stroked, petted. A lot of anxieties and hostilities can be dissolved while petting a purring cat. Animals provide companionship.

Encourage your aging parent to continue working at his or her hobbies or to take up new interests. How about mountain climbing? Ninety-year-old Hulda Crooks hoisted a twenty-five-pound backpack onto her hunched shoulders and set off for the day's activity: to climb Mount Whitney. As if that weren't enough of a challenge, she recently tackled Mount Fuji. Hulda runs too, "because it made climbing so much easier."

I'm certain we've all drunk enough pity party juice to know its drugging effects. One drink of the self-pity cup tips me into a dance of "I wants." One bottle intoxicates and spins me into a reflection pool where I see me, myself, and I. My pain, my misery, my loneliness, my . . . my . . . my. . . .

No age is spared from the heady desire to sample the pity cup. Self-initiated hopelessness drives teenagers as well as adults into mental hospitals and at times to suicide, and the elderly into so-called "senility." We all need to be needed, we all need people around us to pull us out from under the influence of self-pity.

Help your parents look outside of self and into a whole world of people who need them.

Social Contacts

Who needs them? RSVP does. Retired Senior Volunteer Program is a volunteer clearinghouse that places retired people in volunteer jobs with various public and private nonprofit agencies in the country. Look up this great organization in your phone book or check out the address for the national office in chapter 14.

There is a senior citizens' group in practically every community, with every imaginable activity. Peers, especially those with an up-with-aging attitude, can be a great help in lifting a friend out of depression. Check into the senior citizens services available in your area.

In some cases, the despair may be so pronounced your aging parent needs professional help. A medical checkup, with a geriatric specialist, may result in a mental health workup and psychological counseling.

Psychological counseling for the elderly may not be easy to come by. In a *Psychology Today* (January 1984) article, "Therapy After Sixty," I learned that "Less than three percent of the clients treated by clinics or private therapists are older than 65, and as recently as 1981, nearly 70 percent of the clinical psychologists in this country reported that they were not treating any older patients."

Why?

Many of the aging with psychological problems were simply thought to be senile. Some psychologists admit to feeling threatened by elderly patients, thinking, *Am I going to be like that some day?* Fortunately, more and more therapists are recognizing the need in the area of counseling for the elderly.

God Never Said, "Go Retire"

What God said was, "Go, make disciples of all nations." We are asked to do God's will, no matter what our age. Can God use older people? Did God use Moses? Abraham?

Retirement could be a transfer from a "when I get a chance" ministry to a full-time service in God's business. One sixty-three-year-old woman said, "I couldn't stand the thought of sitting around growing mold . . . I mean old. Ha," she chuckled, "when you come right down to it, maybe I was right the first time. Anyway, I decided to enjoy the rest of my life so I joined the Peace Corps. I get more kick out of giving myself away than Christmas. These people really need me. Maybe I need them too."

Not everyone will opt for the foreign mission field, but there are plenty of opportunities to serve in our own communities. It may be tough getting your elderly parent involved. And perhaps he or she is physically or mentally incapable of service. However, even to the end, there may be some task, like snapping beans during canning season or stirring cookie dough or holding yarn, you could assign to give them a feeling of being needed.

Children can make a difference. The elderly without grandchildren or great grandchildren would enjoy being part of the "Foster Grandparent Program." Every child needs a grandparent and every grandparent needs a child.

The suggestions made in this chapter will help your aging parent maintain optimum independence, while assuring safer and more productive living conditions.

There are many sensory and physical changes that can affect the degree of independence your parent has. The aged are more susceptible to medical problems and some medical problems become more pronounced in the elderly. In the next two chapters I'll review those common illnesses and symptoms most likely to plague your aging parents and rob them of their precious independent life-style.

8

Alzheimer's: The Disease of the Century

The definition of Alzheimer's disease (AD)—an irreversible form of dementia—is "The deterioration or loss of intellectual facilities, reasoning power, memory and will, due to organic brain disease . . ." (Blakiston's Gould Medical Dictionary).

Alzheimer's, often misnamed Old Timer's Disease, has received much notoriety of late. In fact, it often becomes a catch-all phrase for any type of dementing illness. Because it has been referred to as "the disease of the century," and because so few people really know and understand the disease, I decided to dedicate a whole chapter to it.

Often lately, I've heard people make statements like, "My mother won't go to the doctor. She complains of being too forgetful and is afraid her doctor will tell her she has Alzheimer's."

There is a comforting piece of advice in a recent publication of the Alzheimer's Disease and Related Disorders Association (ADRDA) by Dr. Benson Schaeffer, a Portland psychologist. He wrote, "Regarding memory losses . . . such losses interfere with awareness. The person who does not remember events, people, places, things, and facts does not remember that he/she does not remember. Partial memories remain, and along with them a partial awareness of incapacities, but complete awareness is usually not possible. This may be a good thing."

Anytime an illness receives as much publicity as this one, people tend to relate themselves to the symptoms. I certainly can understand the concern. As I reviewed the initial symptoms, I thought, *Hmmm . . . could that be me?*

One of the warning signs of Alzheimer's is memory loss—forgetting people's names, important appointments, losing things. Another is the loss of ability to find words and express oneself. Oh dear, am I in trouble. I do forget names and have forgotten appointments. I lose things—boy, do I lose things. And have you ever been at a loss for words? I have. Is it Alzheimer's? Good heavens, I hope not.

We all do strange things sometimes. At least I hope I'm not the only one who's put the milk in the cupboard and the salt and pepper in the fridge. Or, gone into a room and forgotten why. Or, rattled off each child's name before finally getting to the one I was really trying to yell at.

To be honest with you, I'm not really serious about thinking I might be exhibiting the symptoms of Alzheimer's disease. I've been like this since early childhood. For me it's normal and it probably is for you as well.

I'll be telling you about the different phases of the disease and give you a more complete picture of the Alzheimer patient a little later in this chapter, but first a history lesson.

What It Is

Alzheimer's was first described by Alois Alzheimer, a German physician, in 1907, and ultimately named for him. He was caring for a fifty-one-year-old woman who seemed to be exhibiting symptoms similar to those found in elderly patients with *senile dementia.*

Alzheimer's disease comes under the heading, *Organic Brain Syndrome,* a form of dementia with no known cause, prevention, or cure. The victim may experience hallucinations, depression, memory loss, and inability to reason, all the signs previously thought to be natural aging. But many patients, like Dr. Alzheimer's fifty-one-year-old, are not what most of us would consider old.

While symptoms occur that lead physicians to suspect Alzheimer's, there is only one way to confirm the diagnosis—through autopsy. Although a brain biopsy can be done to determine the diagnosis, it is rarely tried because even with a confirming diagnosis, nothing could be done.

In an autopsy revealing Alzheimer's, a physician will find changes in brain structure. These changes include large numbers of *neurofi-*

brillary tangles (delicate protein filaments resembling tangled yarn) and *neuritic plaque* (degenerating nerve cells).

These plaques and tangles destroy brain cells. The progress of the disease varies from patient to patient. But whatever the speed, Alzheimer's pursues a relentless course that leaves its victims unable to reason or remember.

Identifying Alzheimer's

Elizabeth Lincoln in *Managing the Person With Intellectual Loss at Home* (a publication of the Burke Rehabilitation Center) breaks the symptoms or changes seen in the Alzheimer's patient into four recognizable phases. The following information is adapted from her studies and my own.

Phase One: In this often deceiving phase, the subtle onset may leave the family feeling suspicious, but unsure that anything is wrong. The patient can continue to function as long as the environment remains familiar. But even then, forgetfulness interrupts and frustrates daily activities.

The first changes include some memory loss—especially forgetting phone numbers or names, being unable to find the right word or phrase. Loss in spontaneity and less sparkle, energy, drive, and initiative can lead the patient to cover up by blaming his or her problems on fatigue, stress, overwork, or other people. Often in this phase the patient will seem vague and uncertain, slow to learn and react. He or she may become depressed, passive, restless, or easily angered. Awareness of the forgetfulness and knowing that something is going wrong may result in nervousness, anxiety, insomnia, depression, anger, or hostility. The AD victim may express a fear of "going crazy." There will be a preference for the familiar and an avoidance of the unfamiliar with less interest and some indifference to social life which may be mistaken for an "I don't care" attitude.

One family sensed a problem with seventy-three-year-old Ann. Although Ann had exhibited some of the initial changes related to Alzheimer's, the family assumed her memory loss and "eccentric" behavior were a normal part of aging. However, they decided to seek professional help one day when Ann got lost. She had gone to the store, only a block away, for a few groceries. Two hours passed and no

Ann. The family scoured the streets and finally called the police. Authorities found Ann seven miles from home, walking in the opposite direction. Ann had slipped from the vague symptoms of phase one to the more detectable symptoms of phase two.

Phase Two: Some supervision may be necessary during this phase even though the patient may continue to function fairly well. Direction is needed to function in a familiar setting, but the patient can still respond to instruction.

Changes include speech becoming slower, a lack of understanding of verbal or written instructions, and an inability to follow conversational flow. The victim may be unable to reason out math problems—like balancing a checkbook—or to learn new skills. Misunderstandings, increased forgetfulness of the present, indecisiveness, paranoia, inability to perform simple tasks, showing poor judgment (such as leaving a stove on), getting lost in familiar surroundings, and other such symptoms become apparent as the disease progresses. There is greater difficulty in remembering to take medications or pay bills. The victim begins to neglect health, forgetting to bathe and attend to other personal needs. Manners may be poor or completely lacking. All this may cause the family to see the AD victim as lazy or stubborn at first. Then, when they realize it isn't the patient's fault, the family feels guilty.

It might be a good idea to note here that although the Alzheimer patient may seem to be cantankerous or even purposely trying to make life miserable for everyone, that isn't the case. Alzheimer's is a disease. The part of the brain (the cortex) that gives us the ability to reason and remember slowly and progressively dies.

Alzheimer patients don't realize when they're acting in a socially unacceptable manner. One woman began swearing, although she had never used profanity in her life. She didn't want to. Had she known, the truth would have shocked her and she probably wouldn't have believed it. But she, like other Alzheimer victims, had no control over the way she functioned or behaved.

One family felt ashamed and angry over the behavior of the husband/father. In social settings he had become increasingly abusive and insulting. One incident happened at a dinner party. An Alzheimer's victim, Ken, had gone out to dinner at some longtime friends. They had only been there a few moments when Ken became agitated.

"Who are these people anyway?" he questioned his wife. When she realized he wasn't joking, she whispered the names and reminded him of their longtime friendship. He suddenly jumped up and grabbed his wife by the arm. "Come on, we're getting out of here. These people are trying to poison us."

You can imagine the wife's embarrassment and confusion.

At this stage and into the next, the family of the Alzheimer patient become victims of the disease as well, and they may find themselves social outcasts, alone with their bewilderment. They often try to cover up and pretend it isn't really happening.

Sometimes it takes a life-threatening situation to bring the family to the realization that there truly is a problem, and medical or psychiatric help is finally sought.

For example, it wasn't until Ken was found driving the wrong way on the freeway that his family finally faced the fact that Ken was experiencing more than just "crotchety old age."

Phase Three: In this phase there is no doubt the patient is obviously disabled. The patient needs assistance to carry out even the routine activities of daily life. Protection and supervision are a must.

Changes include a more significant memory loss of present or recent past, with an astonishingly clear recall of distant past. The patients can't remember how to act, dress, or use eating utensils. They may shuffle or at times seem glued to the floor, unable to move their feet. While the victims may be able to express themselves in words, there is increased confusion and an inability to understand and remember. They often ask questions over and over and invent words. As the personality deteriorates, you may see a lack of warmth, lethargy, or hyperactivity, with paranoia, aggression, and hostility. The patients may experience illusions and become immodest—may even sexually expose themselves.

Phase Four: At this stage patients require full-time nursing care in order to survive.

In these later stages, Alzheimer's patients experience total physical and intellectual impairment. Symptoms include inability to feed themselves, incontinency, inability to walk, frequent falls (eventually becoming bedridden), inability to recognize friends and close family, or even themselves in the mirror. The patients can no longer speak or write coherently and will constantly repeat words or actions. Seizures become commonplace, response to pain and other stimuli disappears, and patients eventually lose consciousness.

The duration of the disease and the progression from one stage to another depend upon the age of onset. Younger patients generally progress faster. Progression also depends on the health of the individual, their support system, and the treatment of complicating health problems. From onset to death can take anywhere from months to twenty years.

Most physicians will base their diagnosis of Alzheimer's disease on the symptoms and the progression of these symptoms. Alzheimer's disease, as I said before, is just that, a disease. But, primarily, Alzheimer's is diagnosed by what it is not.

What Alzheimer's Is Not

Alzheimer's is not a mental illness helped by psychiatric intervention.

Many diseases and medical problems can cause the onset of symptoms similar to those present in Alzheimer's. By doing extensive diagnostic tests doctors can rule out most of the other possibilities and come to a diagnosis of Alzheimer's.

Dementia is the word most often used to describe the symptoms I mentioned above. The main responsibility of a physician is to rule out a series of other illnesses. This is done primarily because many other causes of dementia can be halted or cured.

Disorientation, confusion, irritability, depression, and other dementia-related symptoms can occur with those correctable problems I talked about in the last chapter—sensory deprivation.

Remember the story of the woman with the overloaded medicine cabinet? Drugs are a common problem for the elderly, especially tranquilizers, sleeping pills, heart medications, arthritis medications, and so on. Nearly all medications are a potential source of confusion for the elderly. I'll tell you more about drugs and the elderly in the next chapter.

The sudden onset of an illness or injury can also bring about mental changes. Diseases the doctor will want to rule out include heart attacks, infections, dehydration, malnutrition, strokes, thyroid problems, vitamin B_{12} deficiencies, diabetes, liver or kidney dysfunctions, and brain tumors or injuries, just to name a few. There are over 100 reversible causes of mental impairment.

It's easy to believe someone really suffers from senile dementia when in fact the disorientation and behavioral changes stem from an entirely different source. Even medical people have a hard time distinguishing the difference.

For example, an eighty-nine-year-old man was admitted to the hospital with a diagnosis of pneumonia. He was extremely confused. Upon further evaluation the hospital personnel discovered that the batteries in his hearing aid were dead. They changed the batteries and talked to him. He opened his eyes, looked around, and exclaimed, "Oh, I thought I was dead."

The poor man had been pushed, shoved, and used as a pin cushion, completely unaware of what was happening to him because he couldn't hear. The result made him disoriented and confused.

Who Gets Alzheimer's Disease?

"Alzheimer's victims come from all ethnic, racial and socioeconomic backgrounds. The disease usually strikes those middle aged and beyond. The youngest known victim was 28 years old. Today it is estimated that more than 1.5 million Americans suffer from Alzheimer's Disease, 10,000 of whom live in the Portland, Oregon, area alone. It is the fourth leading cause of death in this country (next to heart disease, cancer, and stroke), claiming at least 120,000 victims each year." ("What Is Alzheimer's Disease?" a paper by a chapter of the national Alzheimer's Disease & Related Disorders Association, Portland, Oregon.)

According to Patricia Newton, M.D., who spoke at a recent Alzheimer's seminar I attended, "Alzheimer's accounts for probably 50 to 60 percent of those with senile dementia. Twenty-five percent can be attributed to multiple-infarcts (a series of strokes). About 10 to 20 percent have reversible or treatable senile dementia."

While approximately 5 percent of the population over sixty-five have some dementia, the problem increases with age: 10 percent in those over seventy years of age, 20 percent in those over eighty, and 25 percent in people over eighty-five. Alzheimer's accounts for about half the nursing home population.

According to Dr. Newton, of those patients suspected to have Alzheimer's and referred for workup, about 15 percent don't actually have the disease.

Is Alzheimer's Treatable?

There is now no known cure for Alzheimer's, nor any known way to reverse or stop the process of brain cell destruction.

The disease progresses to difficulty in breathing and eventually to paralysis. Death is usually caused by a secondary problem such as malnutrition, infection (like pneumonia), or accident.

Dr. Dennis Selko of Harvard Medical School says, "I think in the next five years there will be a number of other developments that will bring us closer to understanding the mechanism that causes this." Once that happens, scientists hope a treatment and perhaps even a cure won't be far behind.

Researchers have been working on an anti-Alzheimer's drug called THA. According to an article in *USA Today*, August 5, 1987, $5 million has been granted for a two-year study of the drug. While THA is not a cure, it may delay memory loss and slow some physical malfunctioning. For information on this study you may call (800) 621-0379 or for Illinois residents (800) 572-6037.

While this is good news, the unfortunate fact remains that there is no cure for Alzheimer's. Some of the methods of treatment may slow its progression, but for most part, the patient just keeps getting worse.

Family members have described Alzheimer's as "an unending funeral."

"It's like losing a loved one a little at a time. At least in death there's a finality, a once-and-for-all good-bye. With Alzheimer's the loss goes on and on and on."

"Grief begins with the initial decline of body function and mental ability, and it continues through each loss until physical death."

"It's hopeless."

Help for the Hopeless

The medical journals and newspaper articles drip heavy with hopeless grief over the tormented victims of Alzheimer's and their families. In my studies, however, I found a book that gives hope to those "hopeless" families, *Precipice: Learning to Live With Alzheimer's Disease* by Claire Seymour. Claire writes a painful and revealing account of life with her husband, a victim of Alzheimer's. In the book she shares her hope:

> I came to learn by experience that God gives us sufficient strength for whatever may be needed. At times, He seemed to throw a protective veil around my feelings so that I was numb and therefore immune to happenings which would otherwise have overwhelmed me. By shutting off my feelings, He gave me freedom to act in a matter-of-fact way, to be constructive, to get on with the business of living, for life must go on. I also learned that when I come to the end of myself, as I did so often during those terrible four years, the only thing left and the only thing that matters, is my relationship with Him; there is really nothing else. He is the only lasting source of comfort, peace, and strength. He will walk every precipice we meet in our lives with us, if we call on Him. Usually, it is the last thing we would choose ourselves, but He can turn it into growth, maturity, and victory. Victory over fear, over death, over the unknown future. That is not to say we don't suffer physically or emotionally. We do, for we were never promised freedom from sorrow in this life. But there is the inner assurance that all this has been overcome because we have as our guide the creator of the universe—He who is all knowing, all seeing, everywhere present—a God of compassion and understanding who has traveled the same road in human form and identifies with every suffering we shall have to face.
>
> No matter how desperate the journey, then, we are not alone. The absence of joy does not mean the absence of God, for He is just as real in our pain as He is in our joy, even though we may not always feel His presence.

Claire openly shares the painful reality of Alzheimer's. She has learned to cope and offers help and comfort to those who travel the same tragic journey. If you have a family member who suffers from mental illness or organic brain disease, I recommend *Precipice.*

The biggest relief comes to families who know they are not alone. Support groups have sprung up all across the nation to lend a helping hand, to share, to give support and encouragement, to say, "I understand," and even to help bring laughter back into the joyless heart again. You will find a list of the national support groups for Alzheimer's disease and similar disorders on page 174.

Perhaps the biggest question and the one most frequently asked is, "Why? How could God have allowed this to happen?" No matter how long we have believed in God or how deep our commitment and faith, when something bad happens, we ask, "why?"

Forget the old clichés—"God works everything for good," "It'll get better," "Cheer up," or "Look at the bright side"—they only fan the flames of pain, at least until the initial stages of grief have been resolved.

Living through Alzheimer's with a parent or spouse is hell. But when I think about it, the Lord conquered that too. And even now, hope rises like the morning sun as each new day brings us closer to a cure or at least a way to slow this dreaded disease.

From Alzheimer and its related illness of senile dementia let's move on to explore other common illnesses that are most likely to affect our aging parents.

9

Common Illnesses and Symptoms Affecting the Elderly

In the last chapter I talked about Alzheimer's and called it the disease of the century. Remember also, that I said it was the fourth leading cause of death among the elderly. In this chapter we'll learn about the three leading causes of death and other health problems most likely to affect aging parents.

The information here is not meant as a tool for making your own diagnosis or determining methods of treatment. It is solely for your information to help you understand the various illnesses and determine when and if your aging parent requires medical help.

Arthritis

By definition, *arthritis* simply means inflammation or degeneration of a joint or joints. Not so simply, as a diagnosis arthritis includes over 100 diseases.

No doubt you've often heard Gramps grumpin' about his "gout" and Granny spinnin' yarns about her "rheumatiz." Although not all aches and pains in the joints are actually diagnosed as arthritis, many are. In fact, about 30 million Americans have some form of the disease, that's about one out of every eight people, according to author Ada P. Kahn, M.P.H., in *Help Yourself to Health—Arthritis.*

The most common form, *osteoarthritis,* also called "old age arthritis," accounts for about 16 million of the people afflicted with the condition. The diseased joints occur in increasing frequency with age, causing gradual disability. This one is known for the aches and pains and doesn't usually produce inflammation (swelling or redness) or cause general illness.

The second most common form, *rheumatoid arthritis*, affects around 6 million people. It not only inflames joints, but can cause diseases in the lungs, blood vessels, heart, and other organs. It can cripple and even kill. Rheumatoid arthritis ravages all ages. Even in children this debilitating disease may destroy joints and inhibit normal growth.

Symptoms of Arthritis

Most people suffer aches and pains of some sort, but as I mentioned earlier, not everyone has arthritis. Below are some symptoms or warning signs of arthritis designated by the National Arthritis Foundation:

- persistent pain and stiffness when arising
- pain, tenderness, or swelling in one or more joints
- recurrence of these symptoms, especially when they involve more than one joint
- recurrent or persistent pain and stiffness in the neck, lower back, knees, and other joints

Perhaps, like me, you took one look at that list and said, "Oh, my aching back. I've got it." Maybe you do, or maybe your aging parent does, but you can't know for certain unless that "aching back" or body has a complete physical examination and specific tests. In other words, if you or your parent's symptoms are painfully close to those on the above list, don't panic, just make an appointment to see a physician soon.

Myths and Realities About Arthritis

Many see arthritis as a hopeless, nontreatable disease that "you have to learn to live with." In the early 1900s this was true, and the disease brought frustration and hopelessness. Over the past twenty-five years or so, research and a specialized group of arthritis experts called *rheumatologists* have changed all that. Although most forms of arthritis can't be cured, *all* of them are treatable. Treatment includes everything from specific drugs, to diet, proper doses of exercise, relaxation, and even surgery in some cases. Care and treatment vary according to the type of arthritic disease.

One distressing reality is that "while less than $15 million a year is spent on research, victims of the disease spend more than $250 million on worthless and misrepresented drugs and treatments."

Yes, there are treatments for arthritis, but encourage your aging parent to stay away from the "sure cures" and stick to the advice offered by trained medical people.

With television and the easy availability of over-the-counter drugs and treatments, we tend to believe almost anyone who just might be able to relieve our misery "the easy way." The only "miracle cures" can come from God, and I would encourage you to pray for healing and relief from pain, not throw money into drugs whose manufacturers make promises they can't deliver.

One point I might make here is that I see hundreds of different brands of pain medications on the drugstore shelves. Most of them contain either acetaminophen or aspirin (acetylsalicylic acid), or a combination of both. With all the fancy names and promises, many people think they are getting something special. This is a good time to remember, a rose by any other name is still a rose. Likewise, a generic acetaminophen will cost less and do exactly the same thing as Tylenol, Tempra, Aspirin Free Anacin 3, etc., etc., etc. . . . You'll find the same is true with aspirin—the drug most recommended for arthritis. (If your parent does use aspirin, the enteric coated tablets happen to be easier on the stomach.) Check the label before you buy. You'll see that for nearly half the cost you can purchase the same medication. The only things missing are the advertising gimmicks and the fancy names and labels.

More information about arthritis and its various forms are available from the National Arthritis Foundation, 1314 Spring Street NW, Atlanta, Ga. 30309 or from a local Arthritis Foundation chapter.

Bronchitis and Other Lung Problems

Bronchitis, emphysema, and pneumonia are the most common lung problems that affect the aging. One will often lead to another, and the end result for the frail older person may be death.

Bronchitis is an inflammation of the mucous lining and bronchial tubes. The disease may come on as a result of infection or irritation from inhaling harmful substances. When infection causes bronchitis, antibiotics can help. In chronic bronchitis however, the irritant, such as cigarette smoke, must be eliminated. If chronic bronchitis goes untreated it may gradually progress into pulmonary emphysema.

To Breathe Is Life

With *emphysema*, the air sacs in the lungs become damaged, often as a result of heavy smoking. The lungs lose their elasticity and cannot do their job of exchanging oxygen from inhaled air for the carbon dioxide from the blood. Loss of this essential body process results in eventual suffocation. Symptoms usually appear as a hacking, persistent cough and shortness of breath.

My father had emphysema. Watching him work to draw in those precious particles of oxygen in order to live, convinced me of the dangers of smoking and air pollution. I promise not to get on my soapbox and rant about the dangers of smoking and keeping our air clean, but watching a parent slowly suffocate builds a pretty strong defense.

Treatment for emphysema patients may include breathing devices, portable oxygen tanks, medications, and exercises. *Dyspnea*, the fancy word for difficulty in breathing, can affect the entire body since each cell requires oxygen to function. Heart failure, anemia, weakness, and pneumonia are the most common complications.

Pneumonia

Whenever people, especially the elderly, become weak or bedridden, they are extremely susceptible to pneumonia.

Pneumonia is an inflammation or infection of the alveoli (the small air sacs) in the lungs. It can be brought on as a complication of any disease, accident, or problem that makes a person inactive. Difficulty in swallowing can also result in getting fluids or food into the lung accidentally, causing pneumonia.

Although pneumonia can be cured in normally healthy individuals, it often results in death for the frail elderly. Some doctors recommend that people over sixty-five be immunized to prevent pneumonia. Check with your parent's doctor about this.

Any symptoms such as prolonged cough, difficulty in breathing, persistent sore throat, or congestion, with or without fever should be followed up by a physician's examination. If caught early, lung problems may be halted.

Cancer

"Mrs. Rushford, I have the report back on your biopsy. You have a malignant melanoma."

The words churned in my mind. *Malignant—cancer. Melanoma—"a pigmented mole or tumor."* The disturbing mole I'd neglected for months had been growing cancer cells. The doctor went on to explain how he would remove a five-inch radius around the mole down to the muscle, then graft skin from my thigh over the excision.

It seemed like a nightmare, something that was happening to someone else. But cancer doesn't happen just to other people. It can attack anyone.

Who Will Get Cancer?

Contrary to what my youngsters think, I am not an aging parent. Maybe I should rephrase that. If you think about it, any of us with children are aging parents regardless of what age we are. Rather, I am not elderly. And, although cancer mainly affects older people, it invaded my cells when I was just thirty-seven. No matter what your age, cancer is a fearful enemy that to many means death.

Cancer is the second leading cause of death in America. Even more frightening, the American Cancer Society predicts that one out of every four of us can expect to contract cancer in some form.

What Is Cancer?

There are a hundred or more different kinds of cancer, but there is one common denominator. The disease takes over our once healthy cells and turns them against us. The cells forget their jobs and begin the process of multiplying. As the cancer cells increase, they work to invade and destroy the whole body. Cancer acts as its own worst enemy. Since cancer cells aren't communicable (that is you can't catch it from anyone), when they multiply and kill the body they've occupied, they kill themselves in the process.

At one time, cancer killed every victim it invaded, with the exception of those who received miraculous healing. There were no cures, no treatments. And, contrary to what many believe, cancer is not new. In fact, scientists have found signs of death from cancer in dinosaur bones, mummies, and even in fossils of prehistoric plants.

Can Cancer Be Cured?

The one hope we have now is that in many cases, through surgery, radiation, and chemotherapy (the use of drugs) cancer can be slowed, stopped, or even completely destroyed.

The best way to combat cancer is to be educated about the enemy. Know the warning signs, stay healthy, eat right, and have regular physical examinations.

The American Cancer Association publishes a "CAUTION" list of seven danger signals to watch for:

Change in bowel or bladder habits.
A sore that does not heal.
Unusual bleeding or discharge.
Thickening or lump in breast or elsewhere.
Indigestion or difficulty swallowing.
Obvious change in a wart or mole.
Nagging cough or hoarseness.

These symptoms may or may not be signs of cancer. Only a medical exam can determine the cause. At least half of all new cancer cases can be cured. The problem is that in order to provide a cure, the cancer must be found while it's small—before it spreads.

Too often, cancer can't be detected in time. It's been referred to as the "hidden killer," because many times the symptoms don't show until it has grown to serious proportions.

Regular checkups and tests such as Pap tests and breast exams often detect cancer in its early stages.

Since awareness can mean the difference between life and death, you may be the one to make sure symptoms that appear in an aging parent are followed up with a physical exam. You may also need to make certain that appointments for physical exams are made and kept.

Cancer Prevention

Prevention is the best medicine. Many people, through fear and lack of understanding, make the comment, "It seems like everything causes cancer, why try? Why not just eat, drink, and be merry? What will be will be."

Of course there are no guarantees that you will never get cancer if you follow a precise formula, but there are safeguards you can take against the most common kinds of cancer.

How can a person prevent cancer?

1. Don't smoke, and don't hang around people who do.   The incidence of lung cancer is increasing more rapidly than any other type of cancer. Most of those victims will die, and researchers feel strongly it is most often caused by smoking. It seems logical then that people stop smoking. Smoking causes more cancers than any other known agent. It not only causes cancer in lungs, but also in the bladder, pancreas, lips, esophagus, and elsewhere.

2. Eat a well-balanced diet.   Did you know that eating too much fat can cause colon and breast cancers? You don't have to give up everything, including an occasional dessert or a little "junk food." Simply eat what your body requires for good health and avoid too much of any one thing.

3. Avoid chemicals.   Ever check out the chemicals in products we use every day? You can't be alert to every danger, but you can avoid strange smells, chemical dust, or pollutants, such as insecticides, that could invade your lungs or skin. Recently we've learned that some additives in the foods we eat, such as a food dye, Red No. 2, saccharin, nitrite, and sulfur dioxide have been named as cancer-causing agents.

4. Avoid unnecessary radiation.   Don't have X rays you don't really need. Like to tan? Make it gentle, broiling is for meats, not bodies. Too much sun can make your youthful body bronzed and beautiful, but it can also cause decaying skin cancer ten to twenty years later.

5. Seek medical help if symptoms arise.   Last but not least, see a doctor quickly if something goes wrong with your body. No doctor has all the answers and cancer is sometimes difficult to diagnose. An oncologist is a specialist dealing with cancer and its cures and treatments. While you may not be able to utilize the skills and expertise of a cancer hospital or research unit, most doctors should have access to the most current information and counsel from the experts.

For more information about cancer, write to: The American Cancer Society, 777 Third Avenue, New York, N.Y. 10017.

The main feeling I'd like to leave you with as I conclude this section on cancer is hope. I know people who have been healed of cancer, myself included.   Some have been healed through medicine alone. Others have been healed through a combination of medical treatment and prayer. And still others have been healed through prayer alone.

Although I believe medical knowledge comes from God, I wouldn't want to rely on it completely. Doctors don't have all the answers— God does.

Let's face it. Not everyone will be physically healed of cancer. But even though cancer invades and often kills, it can't take away the hope and faith we find in God. Only He can give us strength to face the pain and malignancies (otherwise known as evils) of this world.

Diabetes

Anyone can develop diabetes. So why write about it in a book on aging parents? For two reasons. Diabetes occurs with increasing frequency in those over the age of forty and even more frequently in the obese. Since around 12 million Americans have diabetes, you may be placed in the position of having to help an aging parent maintain control of the disease. In that case you'll need some facts.

What Is Diabetes?

Literally, *diabetes* comes from two Greek words meaning "to siphon" or "to run through." The term describes the vast amount of water loss in urination. Since the urine of a diabetic often contains sugar, a second word is added—*mellitus*—a Latin name for honey, making the full name of the disease *diabetes mellitus*.

In normal body function, sugars (glucose and carbohydrates) provide fuel for energy. What we don't use is stored as glycogen to be used later. The pancreas, a gland behind the stomach, produces a hormone called *insulin* which enables our body to use glucose. Insulin emerges when we've eaten and turns the glucose in our blood to energy and lowers our blood sugar. Another hormone, *glucagon* works oppositely from insulin and serves as a signal for the body to release stored sugar during times of fasting to raise blood sugar.

This balance is one of many that God so intricately created to keep our bodies healthy and in good working condition.

In a person suffering from diabetes, the pancreas either stops working or slows down its production of these hormones. Without insulin the body can't use the glucose it takes in. The result is that the unburned sugar piles up in the blood and finally escapes along with large amounts of water in urine.

Without the balance of insulin and glucagon working to keep our blood sugar at a safe level, we would eventually go into a coma and die.

Symptoms of Diabetes

Because the excess glucose takes along so much water, it is logical that one of the first symptoms is thirst. Also, since the body can't utilize the food adequately, the diabetic will experience hunger and may eat large amounts of food and still lose weight. Then because the insulin doesn't turn the food into energy, the person feels tired, weak, and with less fuel to the brain, may feel dizzy and faint.

The Good News and the Bad News

The bad news about diabetes is that medical science has no cure. Sustaining life means day-to-day, hour-by-hour care and treatment. As the diabetic ages, changes and problems occur that affect nearly all parts of the body. Atherosclerosis (a condition in which arteries thicken and lose their elasticity and shape, and plaques from fat and other materials form, causing constriction to normal blood flow) often shows up earlier in a diabetic. Reduced blood flow through the body impairs other organs such as the heart, brain, kidneys, and legs.

Poor circulation can lead to stroke, heart attack, impaired vision, sores or wounds that become more easily infected and heal slowly. Increased glucose concentration and reduced blood flow may cause blindness.

There are multiple complications for the aging diabetic. The care required is often tedious and continual, but necessary.

The good news is that quality care and treatment can control diabetes and allow the patient a near normal and happy life. In fact the diabetic, who is in constant watch over his or her care, may often boast of better health than a nondiabetic.

Again, if your aging parent is a diabetic, be prepared to help him or her maintain their care or to take over if necessary. Learn all you can about the subject, through your local library or by writing for information pamphlets to the American Diabetes Association, 600 Fifth Avenue, New York, N.Y. 10020.

Heart Disease and Other Cardiovascular Problems

Heart disease has been rated the number one cause of death among Americans. Heart disease is not limited to heart attacks, but also includes other conditions affecting the cardiovascular system.

Atherosclerosis

Atherosclerosis means thickening arteries, loss of elasticity, buildup of fatty deposits. The condition may lead to arteriosclerosis or "hardening of the arteries" (deposits along the blood vessel wall draw calcium and harden). Blood may catch on these hard ledges along the wall, become clots, and plug an artery. If a clot plugs a blood vessel in the brain it results in a stroke, in the heart—a coronary or heart attack, in the lung—a pulmonary embolus. Do those terms sound familiar? It's amazing to me how so many problems evolve around the condition of the arteries and valves. Maintaining life, it would seem, is based on keeping the pump and pipes running free and clear.

Congestive Heart Failure

CHF, congestive heart failure, can occur with any of the above conditions when the heart loses some of its pumping power. When the heart fails to pump adequate blood to the rest of the body, fluids build up. Lungs become congested, producing shortness of breath. Kidneys can't remove water from the blood so the water accumulates. Pressure builds, giving the failing heart more work to do. More fluids back up and pool in the legs and feet. If the cycle is not stopped, the patient could drown in his own fluids.

The drug digitalis is often prescribed to strengthen the heart muscle and force stronger contractions. The congestive heart failure patient may also receive a medication to draw some of the excess fluid through the kidneys and out of the body as urine.

Heart Attack

Remember the buildup of fatty deposits that can eventually close off an artery or release a blood clot? That's where heart attacks begin, not as so many believe, with the pain.

Thousands die needlessly of heart attacks each year simply because they don't recognize the warning signs or symptoms, don't know what to do, or can't get to trained help in time. For your sake as well as that of your aging parents, be familiar with symptoms of heart attack. You can learn what to do at CPR (Cardio Pulmonary Resuscitation) classes offered by the American Red Cross.

The following are symptoms of a heart attack:

- Pain in the center of the chest, just behind the sternum (breast bone). Often this pain is confused with indigestion or heartburn, but is unrelieved by antacids. The pain is often intense or may cause a feeling of pressure.

- The pain may radiate to shoulder, neck, jaw, or arms.
- Sweating
- Nausea or vomiting
- Shortness of breath and perhaps feelings of anxiety

One of the greatest dangers to the heart attack victim is an attitude of pride and denial. In the clinic we've encountered many who insist they're too healthy to have a heart attack. They might say, "It's just a little indigestion." Or perhaps they don't want to make a fuss or, "What if it's a false alarm? I'd be paying all that money out for nothing."

During a heart attack time equals life. Medical help must be sought immediately. Usually, rescue squads respond within minutes; but sometimes even minutes can be too long. That's why I recommend CPR training for everyone.

The sad and yet uplifting part of heart disease is that we can often dictate, by our life-style, whether or not we end up with heart disease. Unfortunately, it is usually not until a person has a heart attack that they realize the importance of reevaluating their lives. Then, when irreparable damage may have already been done, they make the decision to reduce stress, eat right, stop smoking, and exercise proportionately.

Many who do suffer heart attacks and do get help in time can mend and eventually lead fairly normal lives. The incidence of deaths caused by heart disease has dropped and experts relate the decrease directly to changes in habit and life-style.

Heart disease, again, may strike at any age, but it more commonly strikes senior citizens, whose pumps and pipes have accumulated deposits, worn thin, rusted out, and just plain stopped working.

Again, the more you know about the particular health problem, the better equipped you'll be to provide the best care for an aging parent. If heart disease threatens the life and health of your parent you can obtain more inclusive information by writing to your local heart association or to the American Heart Association, 7320 Greenville Avenue, Dallas, Texas 75231.

Hypertension

If a doctor gave the verdict, "Hypertension, or high blood pressure," would you understand? We hear the words often. It seems everyone's second cousin has high blood pressure. Since about 60 million Americans do have it, that isn't surprising. But let's take a brief look at the mechanics of this particular medical problem, and I'll try to answer some questions you might be asking.

To learn about hypertension let's first define *blood pressure*. As the heart pumps blood through the body, pressure is exerted on the walls of the blood vessels. Since you can't feel the blood circulating, it must be measured with special equipment.

A pressure gauge called a *sphygmomanometer* measures the force of blood in the artery in millimeters of mercury (mm Hg). This calibration simply gives us a set of numbers from which to determine whether a person's blood pressure is normal or not.

I'm sure most of you have had your blood pressure taken. A cuff was placed around your arm, and a medical person placed a stethoscope over an artery and listened. You experienced the pressure on your arm as the blood flow was blocked off and the relief as the cuff deflated and blood flowed normally again. What you may not have experienced is the pumping sound heard through the stethoscope.

When I measure a patient's blood pressure, I listen for the first sounds of blood pulsating back through the artery and at the same time read the mercury setting. When the pulsing sounds disappear, I read the mercury line again. The first measurement is called the *systolic* or pumping pressure, the second, *diastolic* or resting pressure. My figures may look like this: 120/88 mm Hg (one hundred twenty over eighty-eight).

Normally blood pressure changes. It may be higher with exercise or stress, lower while resting or lying down. The normal systolic (the first number) is 90 to 140 mm Hg. Normal diastolic ranges from 55 to 90 mm Hg.

Normal is also based on what is right for you. In other words, just because your pressure runs higher than the norm, don't panic. When a blood pressure tends to run unusually high on a regular basis, the doctor will probably choose to treat with medication and recommend a change in diet.

The American Heart Association has dubbed this disease, "the silent killer," because we can't feel high blood pressure and because it can increase the chances of heart attack. In some cases, people with chronic hypertension have complained of persistent headaches, feeling tired, tension, dizziness, and shortness of breath. But these symptoms may not be related to high blood pressure at all. The only way to determine whether or not the condition exists is to have the blood pressure checked on a regular basis.

How Can We Avoid Heart Attack and Heart Disease?

Fortunately, we can reduce the risk of heart attack and disease. How? I'm glad you asked.

1. Stop smoking.   This isn't my soapbox, but that of the High Blood Pressure Information Center of the National Institutes of Health. "Smoking injures your blood vessel walls and speeds up hardening of the arteries. The acute effect of a few cigarettes on blood pressure may be slight, but chain smoking significantly speeds the pulse rate, increases the work of the heart, and raises the blood pressure. People with hypertension should not smoke."

2. Overweight? Lose it.   I know, I know. Losing weight is as easy as not eating. But, for what it's worth, heart disease is more common in overweight people. The right diet can help in avoiding circulatory system problems. Persons with high blood pressure will especially want to watch their salt and/or sodium intake.

3. Reduce high cholesterol.   Again, the fatty deposits settle in the arteries and can cause atherosclerosis. Cutting out the fatty substances or cholesterol can help you lose weight too—another risk factor reduced.

4. Change your life-style.   Want to read it again? Probably not. But . . . eat right, exercise, and take care of your body and encourage your aging parent to do the same. A change just might make the difference.

There is yet another disease prominent among the elderly, that also weaves an unseen thread of danger into our complex circulatory system—stroke.

Stroke

Strokes are the third leading cause of death in our country, next only to heart disease and cancer.

The medical term for stroke is CVA (cerebrovascular accident). Definitions are vague, but generally, it means "a sudden (acute) disturbance of brain function of vascular origin causing disability lasting more than twenty-four hours or death within twenty-four hours."

In other words, a CVA or stroke is caused by a disorder in the blood vessels in the brain. It could be caused by a thrombus or embolus (something that blocks blood flow to a part of the brain) or a hemorrhage (bleeding into the brain from a ruptured or burst vessel).

A stroke may be massive, causing immediate death or disabling paralysis, or it may be slight, causing temporary disability, or something in between. The severity of a stroke depends on the size of the blood vessel involved and its location.

Symptoms include slurred speech; dizziness; severe, sudden headaches; staggering or falling; numbness in extremities.

You know the preventions by heart now, right? You see how important it is to take care of ourselves. What we do in our younger days comes back to haunt us as we grow older.

Other Common Complaints and Symptoms

We've covered the biggest dangers that might interfere with your aging parent's longevity—and yours too. There are other problems and symptoms I'll mention briefly.

Sensory Deprivation

Back in chapter 7, "Maintaining Independence: How You Can Help," I wrote about sensory deprivation and its effects on the elderly.

Be aware of hearing loss, visual changes, decreased sense of touch and smell. See a physician when and if these losses or changes occur and brush up on all the suggestions and information I gave you in chapter 7.

Incontinence

Incontinence means lack of control of the bladder or bowels. It very often affects elderly people. Incontinence causes embarrassment, yet it is a physical problem that in some cases can be treated or cured.

Persons suffering from incontinence should see a physician. In many cases, even if a cure is not available, appliances and/or special clothing may be suggested to solve some of the problems incontinence brings.

You'll read more about incontinence and how it affects the care of aging parents in the next chapter, "Home Care."

Insomnia

In later years the inability to sleep may be the result of anxiety or depression. Or it may be normal. The need for sleep diminishes with age. Did you know that? Yet many take naps and try to get eight to ten hours of sleep at night because they falsely believe they need extra rest. Sleep evades some elderly because they become bored, lonely, or depressed and go to bed very early, then can't understand why they awaken at early hours of the morning, unable to go back to sleep.

Insomnia may be caused by a physical problem, and your parent's doctor should be aware of it. However, if all else is well, you might encourage your aging parent to put that "wakeful time" to good use—read or engage in Bible studies and prayer. If they can't sleep, at least they can make the most of the time.

Loss of Appetite

Appetites vary, of course, in all ages of people. However, an obvious change in eating habits should be reported to a physician.

Poor nutrition is a common problem among the elderly and for several reasons. First, it may be difficult for the older person to shop and prepare meals. Second, they may forget to eat—as many with Alzheimer's do. Third, lack of money may prevent them from purchasing adequate supplies of fruits and vegetables. Fourth, mental instability, such as depression or anxiety may alter eating patterns. Finally, their teeth may need care. Good oral hygiene and dental care can make a difference in appetite and ability to eat.

Not eating properly can precipitate other medical problems, as you've seen over and over in this chapter. Be aware of eating changes in your aging parent. You may need to step in with help from your own resources or obtain assistance from a social service source such as Meals on Wheels. The local county extension agency usually has loads of nutritional information in brochures and pamphlets. Also, I've included more information on nutrition in the next chapter on "you as the primary care-giver."

Overmedicated

In chapter 2 I shared a story of a woman who had become confused because she was taking too many medications.

Medications can be a serious problem for the elderly, not only prescription medications (yes, even those the doctor prescribes), but over-the-counter drugs as well. Something as simple as a cold pill could cause confusion in an older person.

The simplest way to combat an overload of, or a reaction to, any medication is to:

- Keep a current list of all medications taken and when.
- Review that list periodically with the physician.
- Review the list whenever a new drug is added.
- Never use an over-the-counter drug without first consulting a physician. (Be sure to describe other medications being used.)

A Word About Physicians and Health Care Personnel

While the subject of doctors doesn't qualify as a symptom or illness, having the wrong doc certainly could bring on an illness or make a patient worse.

Many of our parents may have the idea that what a doctor—any doctor—says is law. While the majority of doctors may be competent, not all of them are. The same can be said of nurses, pharmacists, and other health care professionals.

It is important that your aging parent have a doctor you both can trust and feel comfortable with. Beware of health care professionals who blame all of the older family member's ailments on "old age."

Make certain your parent's doctor understands the elderly and is sensitive to their needs and problems or who perhaps is a geriatric specialist.

Although there are many more symptoms and ailments that could affect an aging parent, I have tried to give you a rundown on the most common.

Often you will be the only one to notice symptoms that could lead to trouble in your aging parent. Sharpen your assessing skills. Just as you watched for signs of illness in your children, be alert to changes in your parents that might signal a disease or medical problem.

10

Home Care

The patient neither speaks nor comprehends the spoken word. Sometimes she babbles incoherently for hours on end. She is disoriented about person, place, and time. She does, however, respond to her own name. I have worked with her for the past six months, but she still shows complete disregard for her physical appearance and makes no effort to assist in her own care. She must be fed, bathed, and clothed by others. Because she has no teeth, her food must be pureed. Her shirt is usually soiled from almost incessant drooling. She does not walk. Her sleep pattern is erratic. Often she wakes in the middle of the night, and her screaming awakens others. Most of the time she is friendly and happy, but several times a day she gets quite agitated without apparent cause. Then she wails until someone comes to comfort her.

This case study was presented to a class of graduate nurses studying the Psychological Aspects of Aging and appeared in the *Journal of the American Medical Association* in an article by Paul E. Ruskin, M.D.

When asked how they would respond to caring for such a patient, the nurses answered, "frustrated," "hopeless," "depressed," and "annoyed."

Dr. Ruskin continued. "When I said I enjoyed it and thought they would too, the class looked at me in disbelief. Then I passed around a picture of the patient: my six-month-old daughter."

Hmmm. Really gets a person thinking doesn't it? Why should it matter whether a patient is ninety years old or six months? Both should receive the same loving care and compassion. Yet it is definitely more difficult to care for the elderly patient. Why?

"The infant," Dr. Ruskin says, "represents new life, hope, and almost infinite potential. The aged patient represents the end of life, with little chance for growth. We need to change our perspective. Those who are ending their lives in the helplessness of old age deserve the same care and attention as those who are beginning their lives in the helplessness of infancy."

It is with this new perspective that I begin my chapter on home care, with you as the primary care-giver.

People choose home care for a large variety of reasons. These include love and devotion, a sense of responsibility, and lack of money for other types of care. Most of all, I would hope that those of you who choose home care will consider caring for an aging parent a privilege and a joy—not a burden.

Whatever the reason, should you choose to provide care for your aging parent in your home, you're going to need some special skills. Don't panic. You've already learned a great deal about different illnesses and symptoms, and some environmental changes that can make life easier for the older person in your life.

In this chapter, we won't dwell on the independent, or even the semi-independent parent. We'll dwell more on the parent who depends on others for daily care—the one who is convalescing or one who has a debilitating or terminal illness or condition, who does not require acute hospital care.

My husband's grandad, for example, had cancer. He could no longer take care of himself, nor could his wife care for him. But rather than place him in a nursing home, one of his daughters cleared out an extra bedroom, equipped it with a hospital bed, and brought him into her home to provide loving care in a family atmosphere. With the help of other family members, she fed, bathed, and medicated him, and saw to his needs for several months.

The family tried to keep Grandad at home; but he soon became dependent and too heavy for the women to lift and manage. In the end, a nursing home had been their only solution. But they were glad that at least for a while Grandad had been surrounded with the familiar—at home with people who loved him.

Caring for a parent at home is not an easy task. If you intend to take on this responsibility then I'd advise you to be well prepared.

Your first task may be to ask someone, such as a community or public health nurse, or a visiting nurse, to evaluate your home as to the feasibility of home care. You will want to check with your insurance company to find out what medical helps, if any, they provide. For example, with my insurance, Kaiser Permanente, a HMO (Health Maintenance Organization), occupational therapy, physical therapy, and home health care are provided when needed. (For more information on HMO's see chapter 12.)

Second on the preparation agenda is to rearrange the home environment. In addition to the ideas I gave in chapter 7, here are some suggestions that can help.

- Choose a private room for your parent, with good lighting and ventilation.
- Keep furniture to a minimum, floors clear and free of clutter.
- Indoor/outdoor carpeting allows for easier cleanup and a nonskid surface.
- Find a quiet part of the house, near a bathroom and close to the kitchen or dining room, all on the same floor—the street level.
- Provide a telephone for chats with friends or for emergency use.
- Provide books, magazines, radio, or cassettes, and perhaps a television set for entertainment.
- Devise a method (perhaps a buzzer system or bell) for calling for assistance.

Whether or not you've planned to, the family will become the nursing staff, full time. One of the first criteria in home care is to pace yourself.

Pace Yourself

No one—I mean *no one*—works twenty-four hours a day. Yet, that's exactly what many people who care for their aging parents expect of themselves.

As a nurse, I know the exhaustion that comes with giving total patient care. Being on duty eight hours a day can turn me into an emotional and physical wreck unless I relax in between and take time off.

How much more so when you are emotionally involved with the person. If you intend to be nurse and companion to an aging parent, plan for time off How?

- Check into hiring someone from a home health-care facility to come in several hours a day or week.
- Hire a student nurse to help out occasionally. (Believe me, most of them could use the extra money.)
- If several family members are involved in the care, set up a shift and day schedule for routine type care.
- Check into the availability of a day-care facility.
- Some home social services are available at reduced rates through government assistance. These include home health care, visiting nurses, respite care, day care, and meal assistance programs. Check them out.

Learn to Meet Their Needs

In addition to taking time for yourself, I'd strongly urge you to learn some basic nursing skills. Of course, I will include some in this book, but if you feel you need more training, you might want to consider a class in beginning nursing skills (usually offered to those wanting to become nurse's aides) at your community college. Also, in many areas, the American Red Cross offers classes on basic skills for home care. Teaching helps may be available through a community health nurse, or, if you have a HMO insurance program, through their home health service.

You can also learn more about home care from an excellent book by Florine DuFresne, *Home Care: An Alternative to the Nursing Home.* Florine gives her readers step-by-step help in caring for their loved one at home.

Let's think back a minute to that story at the beginning of this chapter. Helpless elderly people require full-time care very much like a baby. As a baby must be fed, bathed, and changed, so, in varying degrees, must helpless elderly parents. Every part of their daily living is left in your hands. Neither the baby nor the aged can survive without our nurturing. The best way to go about the business of taking care of our parent is with a strategic plan.

The Nursing Care Plan

In nursing school, we students developed a patient care plan for each of our patients. On these plans we determined the patient's needs—physical, emotional, social, and spiritual.

Make out a nursing care plan for your aging parent. You'd be surprised at how much insight it offers as you restructure your life to meet his or her needs. You may be saying, "I already know my parent's diagnosis, prognosis, and needs, why should I bother to write it all down?"

Taking the time to do a care plan and updating it periodically can help you set priorities so you can give better, more efficient care. Sometimes writing the facts down on paper, in order and complete, clarifies problems so we can more easily find solutions.

I don't know about you, but if I just let the "Things I have to do list" run rampant in my brain I get anxious and never seem to be in control, nor do I get my tasks accomplished. Strategic planning can help us get things done in an orderly way, and if we're lucky we may even have time left over to play.

Not only will this care plan help you organize specific duties, it will also prove invaluable to those you employ or who volunteer to care for your parent while you can't be there. A nurse friend, whose mother had a stroke, says, "A care plan! What a great idea. Unfortunately, I had to learn the hard way." The plan acts as a comprehensive guide for those to whom you entrust the care of an aging parent.

A sample care plan begins on page 113. Read it through and then fill in the blanks. Come on now, no complaining. I've had to do hundreds, you only have to do one, at least for right now. Use a pencil so changes can be made *p.r.n.*—that's nurse talk for *pro re nata* or "as circumstances may require." (Remember these terms, I may quiz you later.)

NURSING CARE PLAN

GENERAL INFORMATION:

Name_____Nickname_____

Address_____Phone_____

Physician's name_____

In emergency contact_____Phone_____

Close family members and/or friends/Relationship:

_____

_____

_____

Previous occupation_____

Nationality_____Other language spoken_____

Limitations/Problems—Diagnosis if any_____

_____

Able to understand own needs and ask for help. Yes ☐ No ☐
Able to understand/follow verbal instructions. Yes ☐ No ☐
Able to understand/follow written instructions. Yes ☐ No ☐
Check appropriate boxes: Memory loss ☐ Easily distracted ☐
Confused ☐ Disoriented to: Time ☐ Place ☐ Person ☐
Behavioral problems: Hostile ☐ Aggressive ☐ Violent ☐
Wanders ☐ Depressed ☐ Argumentative/Contradictory ☐

Negative ☐ Other _____

PHYSICAL NEEDS:

Assistive devices—Glasses ☐ Hearing aid ☐ Dentures ☐ Cane ☐ Other

_____

Remind to use ☐ Remind to remove ☐ Assist to use ☐
Assist to remove ☐ Other instructions_____

_____

Bathing—No help ☐ Remind ☐ Assist ☐ Supervise ☐ Bathe ☐

Prefers—Bath ☐ Shower ☐ Time: Morning ☐ Evening ☐

Comments or concerns: _____

Eating—No Help ☐ Remind ☐ Assist ☐ Feed ☐

Special diet_____

Likes_____

Dislikes_____

Special needs or problems—Dentures ☐ Food seasoning ☐ Difficulty
chewing ☐ Difficulty swallowing ☐ Special utensils ☐

Comments or concerns:_____

Exercise—Type_____

Frequency_____Duration/distance_____

No Help ☐ Assistance ☐ Supervision ☐ Protection ☐

Assistive devices used—Cane ☐ Walker ☐ Crutches ☐

Other_____

Toileting—No help ☐ Remind ☐ Assist ☐

Special devices needed_____
                              (Catheters, pads, protective liners)

Usual toileting routine/schedule_____

How does he/she signal need to use the toilet_____

_____

Sleep—Usual bedtime_____Usually wakes at_____

Preferred amt. of bedding_____

Preferred night clothes_____

Special problems_____
                        (day/night reversal, confusion, etc.)

Special nighttime needs—Medication ☐ Snack ☐ Toileting ☐ Night-light ☐ Reorientation ☐ Other_____

SPIRITUAL NEEDS:

Religious preference:_____

Religious practices: Church ☐ When_____

Communion ☐ When_____Visitation ☐ When_____

Pastor_____Phone_____

OTHER NEEDS:

Entertainment: TV_____Needs Help? Yes ☐ No ☐
                  (Favorite programs)

Radio_____Needs Help? Yes ☐ No ☐

Reading—Able ☐ Unable ☐ Prefers_____
                               (Bible, magazines, books)

Read to? Yes ☐ No ☐ Comments _____

Telephone—Able ☐ Unable ☐ Needs Assistance ☐

Smoking Yes ☐ No ☐ Times _____ Needs Assistance ☐

Supervision ☐ Where_____

Hobbies _____Needs Help? Yes ☐ No ☐

Social Activities_____
                   (Senior citizens, day care, visitors, etc.)

What other concerns or needs can you think of _____

_____

    I realize a form like this means extra work initially, but it does help you get a whole picture of your parent's needs and problems, doesn't it? And it will lessen the explanation time when you leave someone else in charge. Keep a few blank forms. *File the original,* update it, and make copies p.r.n.

Now that you've completed the care plan, it's time for a few lessons in basic nursing care. Just what you've always wanted, right? Well, because you're so enthusiastic, I'll only cover some bare essentials in each of the needs category. You ready?

Physical Needs

Lesson number one—*this is no time for modesty.* If you haven't seen it all by now, it's about time you did. Yes, there is a time and place for preserving dignity. That's not what I mean. What I do mean is that at times, certain unmentionable parts of your parent's body will need to be not only mentioned, but uncovered, examined, cleaned, treated, and yes, even touched. (Whenever possible have someone of the same sex do personal care.)

It isn't easy to care for your parents in such private and personal ways. But I can assure you it is necessary. Perhaps at first, it will be embarrassing; you may feel like you've been caught watching an X-rated movie.

I'll never forget my first assignment to do a bedbath on a male patient. Although a flushed face may have revealed my discomfort, my professional attitude showed confidence and poise. The, "I've seen it all before" attitude came through only because of my superb acting ability. Inside I felt embarrassed and flustered, like a teen on her first date. But better I grin and bare it than cause additional embarrassment to my patient.

The idea then is not to fake it so much as to put aside your own feelings of embarrassment and concentrate on making the patient feel less self-conscious and more comfortable. Let's go on then to your nursing care responsibilities.

Cleanliness: Good Hygiene and Grooming

Although older people who need care are not likely to get "dirty," they may develop odors from incontinence of bladder or bowel. Bacteria breed quickly on the skin. Fragile skin, constantly rubbed and worn by lying or sitting, needs frequent care to prevent bedsores (known in the medical world as decubital ulcers).

The ulcers form over boney areas where constant pressure breaks down tissue and blood flow slows down. Bedsores can be eliminated by frequent turning and positioning, good hygiene, massage, and lotions. Also, I'd recommend using special "egg carton" foam mattresses, sheepskin pads, and socks as protection to the elbows and heels. These as well as other medical equipment and supplies can be purchased through a medical supply house. Look in your Yellow Pages under Hospital (or Medical) Equipment and Supplies. Sears also has a special catalog featuring home health-care items. Ask for one through your local Sears store.

In addition, the elderly are also likely to neglect their personal hygiene—not purposely, but because of decreased sense of smell, listlessness, forgetfulness, or vision loss. Consequently, your assistance may be as simple as a reminder or as complicated as complete bath care. (Helpful hint: Remember to use little or no soap, as it dries the skin.)

To make bath time more manageable for you and your patient, you may want to look into special equipment from a medical supply house. There are shower chairs, special shower heads and extension hoses, and hydraulic lifts for easy in-and-out-of-bathtub maneuvers. These devices can save your back as well as prevent accidents. People, as well as floors, are slippery when wet. Hospitals where I've worked have these devices available. They're wonderful, and they prevent trauma in both patient and care-giver.

Give special attention to hair, teeth/oral hygiene, and fingernails. These are the most likely to be forgotten by the elderly parent. Although long hair may be a woman's crowning glory, it also takes time. A haircut may be a necessity if the patient or you can no longer handle the task. My grandmother had a beautiful silver grey braid, swirled into a knot at the top of her head. Eventually, it had to be cut. Short hair is easier to clean, comb, and manage for everyone.

If brushing teeth or soaking dentures can't be done by your elderly parent, the job falls to you.

Fingernails provide an excellent place for bacteria to grow. See that hands are washed frequently and fingernails groomed and cleaned daily.

Exercise Needs

No one ever outgrows the need for exercise. Even when people can no longer exercise themselves, someone must help them.

For as long as your aging parent is able, encourage some form of exercise—even if you have to work out side by side. Walking and swimming remain the best all-around exercises and should be maintained for as long as physically possible. Cycling is great and these days it can be done in the privacy of home. For cycling outdoors, a safe adult tricycle can be purchased. Every form of activity, even a music fest with hand clappin', foot tappin' music, can provide stimulation.

When physical disabilities eliminate the ability to exercise actively, someone must step in to develop a passive exercise program.

Every joint, every muscle must be worked or those limbs and muscles atrophy (waste away) or contract (draw up and thicken).

For example, have you ever had your arm in a cast or splint for a few weeks? When the cast was removed, did you notice the difference between that arm and the other? The casted one was smaller, and weak, from lack of use. The muscles felt stiff, hard to flex and extend. If not exercised, the muscles would eventually contract, be stuck or frozen, and you wouldn't be able to move the arm at all.

In the hospital we have an exercise program we call "range of motion" in which we work all the joints three to four times a day to keep them movable.

In addition to exercise, the parent must be turned and positioned properly every couple of hours to prevent bedsores and joint stiffness.

Unfortunately, I can't give how-to instructions on all the different forms of passive exercises and proper positions, that would take a book in itself. But I can tell you how to find a book with illustrations and detailed instructions for various exercises, how to move a handicapped person from bed to chair, to walker, to wheelchair, and positioning with posture in mind. The book *Caring for Elderly People* by Susan Hooker is designed to help people with no nursing skills who want to help older persons help themselves. You may want to check with your insurance company; your policy may cover physical therapy treatments at home. You can ask a therapist to come to your home to give you instructions regarding proper exercise and how to's.

Feed Them Right

Sometimes the older person will forget to eat. Sometimes it's just too much trouble. Your job is to intervene whenever necessary to provide a well-balanced diet. A good diet can provide the essential ingredients for more energy, healthier skin, a more alert mind, and even a sense of well-being.

Here are some rules for good nutrition in the "golden years." Encourage your aging parent to eat:

- Two or more servings daily from the milk group
  Includes: cheese, ice cream, yogurt, cottage cheese, etc.
  Provides: calcium, riboflavin (B_2), and protein
- Two or more servings daily from the meat group
  Includes: meat, poultry, fish, cheese, eggs, dried peas, beans, and nuts
  Provides: Protein, thiamine (B_1), niacin, riboflavin (B_2), and iron
- Four or more servings daily from the bread and cereal group
  Includes: Whole grain/enriched breads, cereals, and pasta
  Provides: carbohydrates, thiamine (B_1), niacin, riboflavin (B_2), and iron
- Four or more servings daily from the vegetables and fruit group
  Includes: citrus fruits, fruit and vegetable juices, green leafy vegetables, potatoes, tomatoes, cantaloupe, strawberries
  Provides: vitamin C, vitamin A, iron, and other minerals

What can these various nutrients do for our parents?

1. Protein—preserves and repairs tissue. Forms antibodies to fight infection.

2. Carbohydrate—provides energy; some fiber to prevent constipation.

3. Fat—provides energy; healthy skin.

4. Vitamin A—for healthy eyes, skin, hair; increases resistance to infection.

5. Vitamin C— promotes healthy gums, skin, helps heal wounds, helps body resist infection.

6. Thiamine (B₁)—aids digestion, promotes a healthy nervous system.

7. Riboflavin (B₂)—for healthy eyes, skin, mouth; helps body use oxygen from the air.

8. Niacin—improves digestive tract and nervous system.

9. Calcium—helps preserve and repair bones and teeth, aids muscle contraction, and helps blood clotting function. (In older people, especially in postmenopausal women, bones lose calcium and become porous. This condition is called *osteoporosis* and may be managed by adequate calcium in diet, or calcium supplements, sunshine, and exercise.)

10. Iron—used in building red blood cells to carry oxygen through the body.

Because the elderly so often suffer a lack of appetite or for a physical reason are unable to eat as they should, vitamin/mineral supplements may be required. If you need help to provide a sound nutritional diet, while staying within the boundaries of physical and health limitations, contact your parent's physician or a public health nurse.

One of the major problems in maintaining good nutrition for the elderly is lack of appetite. You can help by varying flavor, texture, temperature, and appearance of the food you serve. Consider inviting a guest for dinner on occasion, serve a meal with a colorful tablecloth, napkins, and perhaps even a floral arrangement and candles. Prepare small portions. Don't overwhelm the finicky eater with a heaping plate. Daily exercises increase the appetite, whether the workout means a walk or range-of-motion exercises.

Older people who have lost the ability to chew may need softer foods such as fish, cottage cheese, yogurt, peanut butter, eggs, ground meat, and poultry. Vegetables may have to be ground or chopped. Soups, casseroles, and stews are not only appetizing, nourishing, and easy to serve, but save money as well.

Feeding an elderly parent can help meet yet another of his or her needs—the need for social stimulation.

Social and Psychological Needs

We are social beings. The need for others to talk with us, touch us, and respond to us never dies. Even the confused elderly need people contact.

One woman commented to me the other day, "When I take Mother out, a lot of people ignore her. Friends stop and talk with me, maybe even ask, 'How's your mother?' when she's sitting in the wheelchair right beside or in front of me. I wish they'd bend down and give her a hug, talk with her, let her know she still exists. I think some folks are afraid of the elderly. Maybe they think if they get too close they'll catch old age. Mom is lonely enough without that kind of isolation."

A social life, even if it's carried on in the confines of your home, is essential. How can you provide it?

Mealtimes, as I mentioned earlier can provide social stimulation through regularly invited guests, comfortable surroundings, and good conversation.

Social needs can be met as the family watches television, or listens to the radio, or has a Bible study, or party. Provide activities, if possible, with senior citizens groups or day-care centers. Remember any contact with another person provides social as well as mental stimulation.

Be careful on the other hand not to overstimulate. Confused patients may become agitated and difficult to control if too many things are going on. Often the elderly enjoy social life best when it is a part of a routine with few surprises.

Many elderly live with severe communication handicaps—inability to recognize people, aphasia (inability to express oneself). Consequently, those of us who can communicate must make the communication process as simple and painless as possible. Here are some communication helps.

- Get the older person's attention before you speak.
- Listen carefully and give them your full attention when they

speak or try to communicate with you. You can pick up clues to what they're saying by the tone of voice, expression, touch.

- Sit or stand close so that you can talk face to face.
- Express one thought at a time, slowly and precisely. Don't jumble your thoughts or switch subjects quickly.
- Ask questions that require a yes or no answer.
- Understand and acknowledge their feelings. Don't suppress theirs or your own.
- Use touch to communicate.
- Don't talk down. Speak adult to adult.
- Involve them in discussions whenever possible.
- Always give reassurance and encouragement.
- Repeat when they don't seem to understand, using different words or phrases.
- Use reality orientation.

Reality Orientation

Reality orientation is just another pretty phrase tacked on to a special program designed to keep the elderly oriented as to time, place, and person—to the reality of life.

Frequent reminders both visual and verbal tell the older person what day it is, where and who they are, and who other people are. A large calendar showing the day, date, month, and year should be clearly visible. A large-faced clock helps an older person stay oriented to time. When you give care, talk about the day, the time, weather. Pictures can help them remember family members. Give reminders if necessary about where they are, who they are, who you are, and who their visitors are. Repetition helps the forgetful or disoriented elderly remain in touch.

No One Ever Said It Would Be Easy

Meeting a parent's needs depends on each one's individual problem. Every illness carries with it a certain set of home care instructions. Be sure to check with your parent's physician about any special treatments or restrictions.

I had suggested earlier that you might want to take a basic nursing skills class at a local Red Cross office or college. Did I hear a loud groan? Want to reconsider? Taking care of an aging parent at home, especially when he or she requires constant care and supervision, can be much like changing four tires at once in a driving rainstorm.

I don't mean to make the situation seem impossible. I know many who have brought a parent or parents into their home. In fact I know two families with three aging parents living with them—at one time.

My friend, Roger, invited his parents—a mother with Alzheimer's and a father who doesn't accept or understand his wife's illness—and his wife's mother to live with him, his wife, and children. "Sometimes," Roger says, "I have to come home from the office to straighten things out. Actually, Mom, the one with Alzheimer's, is easier to handle than my dad. I can usually calm her down by getting her to talk about the past. Dad just gets depressed and angry because she doesn't recognize him and he can't (or refuses to) understand why."

Bringing parents home, whatever the reason, won't be easy. Your life will change. Jenny had to set her own life on simmer when she brought her mother home. "I thought Mom couldn't last another year. She's been with us for ten and is still going strong. We hadn't expected it. Our lives revolve around her needs. But that's okay. Hers revolved around mine for many years while I took the time to grow up."

What are the criteria for home care?

1. Know what you're getting into. Draw on that supernatural strength that comes from faith in God.
2. Plan to put your goals and ambitions on hold. Home care takes time and effort on your part.
3. Plan for extra help. Take time off.
4. Know that your decisions are not set in concrete. You can make changes. In fact, plan with several options.
5. Learn all you can through books and classes so that you are well prepared and able to give the job your best effort.
6. Do what is best for you and your family. Not everyone is called into nursing service, but you may be.
7. Remember, placing an elderly parent in a nursing home is not a sin.
8. Consider the joys and rewards of loving someone so much that

you would give up everything for that person. In her book, *Home Care,* Florine DuFresne shares this:

I have never regretted my decision (to keep my husband home) and count those three years as a time of learning and of satisfaction in fulfilling an important commitment. I believe I grew in love and maturity, not in spite of but because of the challenge of each day . . . One doesn't look for ease but for reasonable solutions to every problem, and the ultimate satisfaction of having brought comfort and help to a loved family member.

This final thought brings the chapter to a close and opens the door to the next where we'll explore ways to care for an aging parent in a nursing home setting. Yes, I did say "care for" them. Did you think that placing someone in a nursing home relieved you of your responsibilities? On the contrary. While most of the nursing skills are left to the staff, you will be responsible for meeting those really important needs such as compassion, understanding, and love.

11

Nursing Home Care–Your Role

With advancing disease there may come a time when people are less important to the patient than the service that they provide.

The physical needs and their satisfaction are nearly the only things that matter. At that point a nursing home is preferable. Consider these things. In a good nursing home, there is someone in constant attendance—someone who is not exhausted, and someone who has relief because he does this work only eight hours a day. It is his professional duty to see to the patient's needs in a cheerful, confident manner without sorrow or anger. I submit that when the patient is no longer able to perceive others as individuals, he is safer and more comfortable with a professional than with his family. (James Haycox, M.D., *New England Journal of Medicine*, July 17, 1980. Used by permission.)

When Do You Consider Nursing Home Care?

Dr. Haycox answers in part the question of when to consider nursing home care. He's referring, of course, to conditions in the later stages of patients suffering from senile dementia such as Alzheimer's disease.

There are other reasons for considering a nursing home.

1. The older person needs full-time supervision and has chosen a nursing home facility over home care. Does that surprise you? Many elderly who suffer from stroke, chronic illness, fractures, heart disease, terminal illness, or who require rehabilitative care actually choose a nursing home over living with a family member. Why?

One women, Ethel, eighty-two, moved into a nursing home when she needed close supervision and rehabilitation after fracturing a hip. "My children have enough to do without looking after me. Besides, I know I've made the right decision. The patients here need me. I talk with them, read to them. And, I know it wasn't fate that led me here. I bring these poor people love, hope, and companionship. I tell them about God. No, it isn't a resort, sometimes the food's as appetizing as a pile of sawdust, but here I'm helping others, instead of others always helping me. I wouldn't trade places with anyone, not even the queen."

2. *Family members are not available to provide home care and the aging parent has nowhere else to go.* Perhaps the aging parent lives alone in a separate city or state, or the family members work and cannot make the necessary arrangements for home care, or the family home cannot accommodate the elderly person who needs medical care. There are many varied personal reasons for choosing nursing home care.

3. *The doctor may recommend nursing home care because he feels his patient will recover more quickly under the close supervision offered in the nursing home.*

4. *The family relationships may be strained, producing high levels of tension and stress on both the care-giver and the patient.* Healing of relationships often stands a better chance when both parties are rested, and not around each other for what often seems like thirty-six hours a day.

5. *Cost.* For some private paying residents, the cost of a nursing home facility may be completely out of reach. But for others, who qualify for Medicaid, Medicare, welfare, veterans programs, or private insurance, the cost may be minimal. You'll learn more about these financial aid programs in the next chapter on finances.

Reasons vary. Each family must reach its own decisions based on the physician's counsel; the patient's diagnosis, condition, response, and financial situation; and the family's feelings and abilities. Neither the home care nor nursing home care decision is permanent. Be flexible and make decisions based on family and individual needs.

What Is a Nursing Home?

Now, let's define a nursing home and dispel any medieval myths that might be floating around. First of all, nursing homes are not *home.* They are institutions. Paid employees operate them and provide care.

According to the Hillhaven Corporation, which operates nursing homes throughout the United States, "Nursing homes are health facilities licensed by the state to provide long- and short-term medical services according to the directives of a patient's physician and with standards of quality set by the state and the facility. Nursing homes are staffed by professional and trained personnel under the direction of a licensed nursing home administrator. Facilities deliver a variety of medical and social services to their patients."

Residential care facilities, also known as *rest homes, adult care homes,* or *homes for the aged,* are not nursing homes. While they do provide help with activities of daily living and social activities, and attend to health needs, they are nonmedical facilities.

We've all heard horror stories about nursing homes. Many of them are true. However, the unsanitary conditions and poor or abusive care are, for the most part, a thing of the past. Even though the best facilities are not luxury hotels, they provide adequate and, at times, even quality care.

In the last few years, a senior advocate organization called the Gray Panthers set about to clean up nursing homes and improve health care for the elderly.

Nursing homes must meet government standards. And most nursing homes are run by competent caring people who specialize in geriatric care.

Within the nursing home care facility you will find a variety of services offered by what professionals call a health care team. Should you choose a nursing home, this total support team will work with you to provide the best available health care for your aging parent. The team includes physicians; nurses: RNs, LPNs, LVNs, nurse's aides; dietary specialists; an activities director; social service workers; housekeeping and maintenance personnel; physical and rehabilitation therapists; and administrative personnel.

Although poorly run facilities are diminishing, in some "homes" for the aged and chronically ill, conditions fall below government standards. Even now, we occasionally hear about nursing home closures caused by failure to comply with regulations.

Consequently, when a nursing home is being considered for a loved one, you will want to make certain that home passes the test.

Choosing a Nursing Home

A successful choice comes when you match what the home offers to your parent's specific needs. Here is a guide to help you.

1. Decide what care is needed.   Consult with your parent's physician about this. For example: Is daily nursing care and routine medical treatment necessary? Does the aging parent need help with personal care? Does he or she require a safe, supportive environment? Does the patient need rehabilitative care?

2. Consider the types of nursing homes available in your area.   There are primarily two different kinds.

The *skilled nursing home* offers twenty-four-hour nursing and other health care. This is used mostly for chronically ill or convalescing patients.

The *intermediate care facility* offers less intensive, but regular nursing care, ensuring daily nursing services and personal assistance in activities of daily living.

Often both kinds of care operate within the same facility.

3. Evaluate several homes.   You may want to do some preliminary footwork with your fingers walking through the Yellow Pages. When you have narrowed your list down to half a dozen, make an appointment. Then, when you visit:

- *Talk with the administrator.* Check the license of the home and the administrator. Ask for a list of basic fees and cost of extra services. (The Department of Health and Human Resources offers a checklist for persons looking into nursing home care. It can keep you from overlooking some important details. You'll find the checklist on page 188. Take it with you when you evaluate the homes.)

- *Ask to see a copy of the "Patient's Bill of Rights."* Is it posted where all the residents can view it? It should be. You'll find a copy on page 186.
- *Meet with the staff and residents.* Look the place over. Is the staff friendly and involved? What is the general attitude of the attendants? How do they relate to the residents as they show you around? Observe the general tone of the place.
- *Use your senses. See* how residents act and are treated. *Smell*— nursing homes do not have to smell bad. (However, sometimes during morning care, if there are many incontinent patients odor may be present.) *Hear* what staff and residents are saying and listen for the tone of voice. *Taste*—Sample the food, if possible. Although institutional food will never be as good as home cooking, it may be acceptable. Compare it fairly—with food served in hospitals and airplanes rather than at home.
- *Tour the facility and grounds.* How is the environment? Check for cleanliness, comfort, convenience, and safety.
- *Ask whether transportation is available*—to visit family, or attend religious services and other social functions.
- *Find out all you can.* Make certain all the special services your parent requires are available.

4. Consider the cost.   While economical for the services and type of care they provide (about 60 to 80 percent lower than acute hospital care), nursing homes can be expensive. Write down the basic costs on a monthly basis for room, food, and nursing care. Then evaluate additional costs for special services including physician's care, therapy, and drugs.

Find out if your aging parent is eligible for financial aid.

5. Once you've made a choice, investigate.   Talk to people whose family members reside in the home, and to the residents themselves.

Ask social service agencies, check with the Better Business Bureau. Review your checklist on choosing a nursing home (page 188).

You'll want several copies of the checklist, one for each nursing home. In addition to the questions asked on that list, I've added a few considerations of my own:

Check laundry facilities. Does the service cost extra? You may want to consider doing the laundry for your elderly parent. There is less wear and tear on the clothing and it comes out fresher and lasts longer.

Find out if the home has a resident chaplain or if there is a ministry for the elderly—Bible study, prayer times, chapel, religious services. Ask where? When? Who? What? Why? If not maybe you or someone from your church would like to offer your services. The highlight of Grandma's Sunday came in the afternoon when a man from a local church came and led them all in old familiar hymns.

Does the home offer a reality orientation program? The better homes do. If and when you choose a nursing home, ask to sit in on a reality orientation class. Most facilities appreciate the family taking part in the patient's care.

You may have other questions. Write them down. Don't be shy about interviewing the staff and administrators of the nursing home. If I owned a fourteen-carat diamond and wanted to place it with a firm for safekeeping, believe me, I'd ask all kinds of questions. Wouldn't you? How much more significant is the task of entrusting our invaluable treasure—an aging parent—to the nursing home.

Besides, you'll find the better nursing homes will be more than willing to answer your questions. They, after all, have nothing to hide.

Since you can't tell what a facility is really like until you've tried it, I suggest you give the nursing home a trial run of about three to six months. Enter the program with an open mind and the reassurance that if it doesn't work out you can revert to Plan A or whatever.

When the Choice Is Made

Once you've chosen a nursing home, you'll have a whole new set of obstacles and dilemmas to face and overcome. You thought the hard part was over? Sorry. We've only begun.

The contract. You or your parent will probably be asked to sign a contract before admission into a nursing home. Before you do:

- Understand what costs and services it covers.
- Have a lawyer (preferably one who has experience with problems of the elderly) and/or financial advisor review it with you.
- Understand it thoroughly—ask questions if you don't.
- Realize that while not every nursing home resorts to fraudulent activity, some do. Protect yourself and your parent.

Canceling Guilt

This is as good a place as any to deal with any underlying guilt that may have worked its way to the surface over this nursing home business.

If you feel guilty, remember that while the nursing home may be the last resort for your aging parent, it is nonetheless an acceptable alternative.

Would you feel guilty if Grandpa fell off his skateboard and you took him to a hospital emergency room for needed medical care? Of course not. Then why do we feel so guilty at the thought of allowing the nursing home staff to care for a parent who needs extensive care?

The main reason for true guilt is desertion; not continuing on as a care-giver. Desertion of an aging parent who needs you will bring guilt running full force—and it should. Remember, true guilt is God's way of saying, "Wrong way—try again."

It's easy enough to fall into this guilt trap. Rose Adams had to place her chronically ill mother in a nursing home. She became extremely depressed at seeing her mother deteriorate and felt overwhelming guilt about having placed her in the home. Rose rationalized that the feelings of despair and guilt diminished when she avoided her mom and kept busy with her own life; consequently, her visits decreased. Then each time Rose did visit, the guilt and sorrow became even more burdensome. Eventually, the visits dwindled to once a month or whenever she could summon up the courage.

Initially Rose's guilt fit solidly into the false guilt category. Her diminishing involvement with the woman who needed her pushed that guilt into the real thing.

What if the parent lives far away and you can't make frequent visits? Here are two solutions: One, bring your parent into a nursing home near you; or, two, send frequent letters and pictures to show you care. And make certain someone checks on your parent regularly.

Another "biggie" on the guilt scene is the aging parent who whines, complains, yells, becomes wholly obnoxious and manipulative every time you visit. The goal is to get you feeling so guilty, you'll take them home. Yes, you should investigate complaints. The care may be lacking. But if you know your parent is well cared for, and the decision is for the best, for all concerned, then tell guilt good-bye and don't look back.

Decide there is no reason to feel guilty. You are after all still caring for that parent. You have merely placed your loved one in the hands of nursing home personnel who make it their business to nurse the elderly. You are still a care-giver. One of your first roles then is to help your parent make the transition.

Making the Move

Making the transition from home to nursing home can be traumatic, especially if the elderly person doesn't want to go. Most nursing homes have pamphlets available to let their patients know just what to expect. Unfortunately, much bad press has given nursing homes a bad name. People are often afraid from early on that they'll "end up in one." When they do . . . well, you can understand their apprehension.

The best way to make the move easier is to plan ahead. Try to anticipate questions. Discuss concerns openly and share decisions. Give the older person (if possible) a part in selecting the home.

Take as much time as necessary to move your aging parent into the new and strange environment. Plan to spend the entire day together. Discuss possible problems, questions, or concerns. The social services or activities director can often help make the move smoother.

Reassure your parent you are not deserting him or her. Plan ahead for several visits or outings. Look through the week's scheduled activities.

The greatest fear of the person placed in a nursing home is that of being mistreated by the staff or abandoned by family. Your job is to alleviate those worries. You do that by frequent and regular visits, and by meeting those needs the nursing home cannot. Be your aging parent's advocate, seeing that his or her rights are not violated.

Remember, no matter how good the facility is, it can't and won't cater to every whim. The care received in the nursing home will, in most cases, never compare with the dedicated care received at home. After all, the nursing staff are not family. Consequently, you remain an essential part of the health care team.

How You Can Help

Now that someone else has taken over the heavy tasks of providing that routine care and halted the burnout you may have experienced while meeting needs twenty-four hours a day, you can finally give your parent some prime time. Use this quality time to provide empathy, maintain dignity and honor, give respect, remind your parent how to smile, laugh, and pray—do all those special things that say without words, "I love you."

This may all seem complicated, but it's simply a matter of being your parent's care-manager. In other words, make certain your parent is well cared for. One of your first jobs as care-manager is to communicate. Be open and honest with staff members. Give praise when deserved and share concerns or problems. Listen to your parent and provide stimulating conversation.

What Do You Say After You've Said "Hello"?

Wouldn't this be wonderful: You walk into the room and your aging parent waves a greeting and smiles. Then a stimulating, pleasant conversation ensues. After an hour of loving care and joyful chatter, you leave feeling refreshed and satisfied.

Unfortunately, life rarely blesses us with *ideal* situations. Somehow, at least in my case, God usually allows me to suffer various trials to give me a chance to learn patience. You too?

Let's take a look at the more real, not ideal, scene. Most often when visiting an elderly parent, we're faced with the problem, *What do I say after I've said, "Hello"?* Here's a technique that might help you.

Enter adult child named Laura. "Hi, Mom." With a Pollyanna

smile, and an armload of treasures, Laura is hoping for a happy visit. Her mother suffers from multiple chronic illnesses, with some senile dementia. As Laura approaches her mother, reality hits. No one has told Mom to have a happy day.

"Get me outa this place before they kill me," Mom growls.

Undaunted, Laura places a kiss on Mom's cheek, squeezes her shoulder. Under her breath she mutters, "Oh no, not again." But with a genuine look of concern, she answers, "You seem upset this morning. Want to tell me about it?"

"Hummph," Mom grumbles. "A lot you care, putting me in a place like this. They didn't even feed me this morning. I haven't had a bath in a month. I want to go home."

Laura makes a quick assessment. *She's clean, smells fresh, hair combed, maybe she really is hungry.* So Laura zeros in on one complaint. Aloud she says, "I'm sorry you're unhappy. I'll go ask the nurse about your breakfast." Laura smiles reassuringly at Mom and gives her a hug. "I'll be right back."

Laura checks out the complaints with the head nurse. She knows most of Mom's charges are exaggerated. According to Nurse Wilson all complaints are invalid except one.

"Yes, she did miss breakfast. After she threw the tray on the floor and yelled, 'Take that garbage out of here. Are you trying to poison me?' we thought it best to wait a while." The nurse added, "Would you like a snack for her?"

"No, that's okay. I brought her some fruit and cheese." On the way back to Mom's room, Laura mutters, "Lord, give me patience. Help me remember that she's sick. Give me the right words to say."

"I talked with the nurses, Mom," Laura said. "They're sorry you missed breakfast." Then before her mother could reply, she continued, "Remember that old peach tree in the front yard? I brought you some fresh peaches. Picked them this morning. Doesn't that sound good?"

Her mother's expression softened, and Laura continued in an effort to turn her mother's thoughts to a happier time. "I'll never forget the day Uncle George got stuck in that peach tree . . ."

Laura's thoughtfulness and sensitivity turned what could have been a sour-grapes encounter into a peaches-and-cream delight.

While not all of you will have to deal with a negative, uncooperative parent, the following tips might help stimulate happier, more satisfying visits.

- *Listen attentively to complaints.* Check them out by talking with the staff and coming in at different times of the day or week to see for yourself whether or not they are valid. Limit the time spent on complaints by moving the conversation on.
- *Stir up positive memories.* Often past recollections remain vivid even though present memory fades. Encourage storytelling. If your parent is unable to talk, share stories with him or her.
- *Bring humorous stories or simple jokes to share.* Use laughter. Remember, "A cheerful heart does good like medicine, but a broken spirit makes one sick" (Proverbs 17:22 TLB).
- *Share news of family members and projects.* Bring pictures.
- *Talk about news topics that would interest your parent.* Remember, a person will probably have the same interests at eighty as they did at thirty. If Aunt Martha loved politics in her youth, she may still want to keep up with political affairs at eighty-four.
- *Whenever possible take the elderly person outside for your talks.* Nature and fresh air lift the spirit naturally.
- *Bring the children.* While outdoor visits may be the best time for bringing the children to visit, I would encourage you to let them come, any age, any time. The residents love it. After all, doesn't the sound of a child's voice, a giggle, and child's play make you smile?

The Comfort and Care Clause

Your entire visit doesn't need to consist of incessant conversation. Some of your best communication may come through silence. This is a part of nursing home care I call, "the comfort and care clause." It's made up of all the special little things we adult children can do to make our aging parents feel cared for and loved.

For example, maintain excellent skin care. Check skin condition on every visit. Once a day or every time you visit, bring a tape of easy listening, inspirational music—classical, romantic, anything soft and mellow. Along with the tape bring oil or a soothing lotion with a soft, pleasant (not overwhelming or perfumed) scent. Pure unadulterated oils such as olive, almond, or safflower lubricate and nourish the skin.

And now, the ultimate massage. What a great way to end a visit. I say end, because by the time your masterful hands are through you will have put your parent to sleep.

Begin at the neck and shoulders. Then move to the back, concentrating on any red or boney areas. Be sure to catch the elbows and knees. Now we're ready for the feet.

Ever had anyone massage your feet? Ahhh. Nice.

Massage not only feels good and promotes relaxation, it stimulates circulation in the skin and helps to prevent bedsores. Since an older person's skin dries easily, use lotion or oil to replace moisture.

Touch tells us we are human, accepted, and desirable. Both you and your parents will find it much more rewarding than sitting around trying to think of something to say.

Some of you might be a bit reserved when it comes to touching. That's understandable. Some cultures express their affection and concern through touch while others remain untouchable. While it's true, not everyone wants to be touched, I've never had a patient turn down a backrub yet—and I've been a nurse for a long time.

Touch is therapeutic. If you don't believe me, try visiting once without touching at all. The next visit try it my way. Then notice the difference in your parent's attitude and temperament. I promise, I won't even say, "I told you so."

By the way, you might let your kids in on this wonderful therapy. Train them now and you'll have an experienced masseur or masseuse when you need one.

Other Personal Needs

Giving the ultimate massage is not only good therapy, it provides you with an opportunity to make observations about your parent's overall condition and gives clues as to the quality of care he or she receives.

Remember all the areas I covered in the previous chapter on home care? All the care provided at home should be given in the nursing home as well. While you will not be doing all the work, you are responsible for seeing that adequate care is given. In addition to the skin, check the eyes, ears, teeth, hair, fingernails, and toenails. These areas are the most likely to be passed over or forgotten by a busy staff.

- *Make certain that eyeglasses are labeled and used.* It is not uncommon for aides to forget.
- *Ditto for hearing aids.* Replace batteries p.r.n.
- *Check teeth or dentures during each visit.* Find out if and when dental care is offered. If it is not, arrange for it.
- *Make sure exercises are regularly scheduled.* Make visiting time exercise time as well. Don't expect a full Jane Fonda workout. Just bring some hand clappin' foot stompin' music and encourage active listening. Encourage other residents to join in too.
- *Ask for a copy of the next week's menu.* Be alert to the quality of the food served. You may want to provide a daily vitamin/mineral supplement, fresh fruit, and nutritious snacks. Also, pop in at mealtimes occasionally to observe how the nursing staff treat your parent. Is sufficient time given for the meal? Are they being assisted if necessary?

Clothing Needs and Care

Clothing done in commercial laundries often comes out looking like leftovers from a rummage sale. Missing buttons, broken zippers, split seams, and worn fabric soon make the nursing home patient's garments ready for the rag pile. The trouble is they don't go in the rag pile; they continue to hang around on elderly patients.

I would encourage you to do laundry for your aging parent along with your own. The garments will come out so much nicer and last longer. Make certain if you do the laundry you're not charged with a laundry bill from the nursing home.

Here are some important things to remember about clothing for nursing home residents:

- The nursing home seldom provides a mending service.
- Synthetics may be easy care, but they provide less warmth in winter and are uncomfortably warm in summer. Cottons and wool blends make the older (and often colder) body more comfortable. This is true of dresses, shirts, pajamas, and hosiery.

Flannel nightclothes, cotton or wool hosiery, cotton or flannel day dresses or shirts in pleasing patterns and colors can make your elderly parent comfortable in both style and temperature.

• Normal garments are often difficult to put on and take off. For comfort and convenience, clothes should be loose fitting, with back openings. As I mentioned before, there are clothing manufacturers and individual seamstresses who specialize in making garments especially for the elderly (see addresses on page 178). You can, however, alter clothing yourself. Slit dresses, shirts, and robes up the back. Face with velcro, or snaps, on the top ten to twelve inches. Sew the front of the garment closed.

• Legs can become cold when a person sits in a wheelchair for several hours. Afghans or quilted lap robes add color and a feeling of home and, of course, warmth.

How you choose and maintain clothing can make the difference in your older parent's sense of dignity, worth, and comfort.

Meeting Mental and Emotional Needs

Empathize. This word means to get inside another person and feel their sorrow, pain, frustration, humiliation, fear, and anger. Not everyone has the ability to empathize. Yet I'm asking you to do it now.

Imagine yourself in a nursing home.

Would you want someone to listen to your problems and complaints?

How would you feel if the nursing assistant talked to you in baby talk? "Are we ready for our bath?" Or made you wear a bib? "Here, Sweetie, let's put our bib on so we don't mess up our new dress." Or, what if they kept your box of Pampers on the dresser top for all the world to see?

Would you like to be referred to as "the hip in 101," or, "the kidney stone in 406A"? How would you feel about being exposed while the aides changed your bed, leaving the door open?

How long would you tolerate a roommate who howled all night, robbing you of much-needed sleep night after night?

Imagine needing help to go to the bathroom during the night. You ring for the nurse, but no one comes. You hold it as long as possible, then. . . . Would you feel humiliated? Embarrassed?

These are all valid complaints, and there are many more. Sometimes the staff in hospitals and nursing homes forget patients are people. There is a tendency when caring for the ill to treat them as children or patronize. Nursing staff may need to be reminded that the elderly are not children but adults with feelings.

Learn empathy.

You Can Make a Difference

By visiting your parent frequently, you not only show care and concern, you will be more aware of specific needs and problems.

You can play an important part in supporting legislation that improves the quality of care and enforces stricter laws regarding nursing homes. I'd encourage you to support organizations such as the Gray Panthers and other patient advocate groups.

Many nursing homes have a Resident Council, which operates within the nursing home. Members are elected by the residents. The council meets regularly; has input into the nursing home policies, state inspection, and federal standards; facilitates communication among residents, staff, families, administration, and the community; and can help resolve grievances.

The manual *How to Establish a Resident Council* can help you understand what this group does and how it is maintained. It is available by writing to the Federation of Protestant Welfare Agencies, Division on Aging, 281 Park Avenue South, New York, N.Y. 10010.

The Department of Health and Human Services assures that nursing home residents receive fair treatment. A public agent called an ombudsman (NHO) may be called in to investigate complaints. For more information write for the manual *Ombudsman for Nursing Homes: Structure and Process*, U.S. Department of Health and Human Services, Administration on Aging publication #78-20293, 300 Independence Avenue, S.W., Washington, D.C. 20201.

The elderly do have rights. And you are the patient's advocate. If any of those rights are abused, you can and should file a complaint. Voice your complaints first to the one who did wrong. If that does not bring about change, go to the nurse in charge, then to the administra-tor, to the department of health, and the agency on aging in your state capital. Go all the way to the top if you must.

You can make a difference in the care your aging parent receives and in the care received by other nursing home residents as well.

12

Finances and Legalities

Even though learning about money and legal problems in regard to our aging parents may appeal to us as much as a trip to Iceland in December, it is important. We would be foolish not to learn about potential problems and how to avoid them.

What I've done in this chapter is to furnish explanations and establish guidelines that can make the whole area of money matters and legal responsibilities uncomplicated and give you a slight headache rather than a throbbing one.

The first problem we encounter is whether or not to interfere with our parents' legal or financial life. This is a delicate situation. Some parents will welcome your concern while others will accuse you of trying to take their money—and resent your interference.

Ideally, it's wise for families to be open with each other—even in the area of wills and finances. Planning ahead and talking over possible problems beforehand can eliminate heartaches and empty pocketbooks.

One of the first items to discuss with your parents is insurance.

Insurance

Too many of us learn the hard way when it comes to the right kind of insurance. For instance, after my dad died, we examined his insurance policies. One policy, which had been purchased many years earlier, paid nothing. The fine print indicated the only way to collect was through accidental death. The policy narrowed eligibility down even further. The policyholder had to be gored by a bull, or lose his life in a boiler explosion on a train or ship.

It's true. Dad thought he had a valid life insurance policy, when in fact he had only a worthless document. With the "lump sum death benefit" from Social Security of $255, and the VA benefits, we had barely enough money to cover funeral costs. I wish we'd have talked about insurance years before. (The *lump sum death benefit* may be available to a surviving spouse who resided in the same household, or to dependent children. In order for the family to qualify for this benefit, the deceased must have contributed to Social Security. Check with the Social Security office for more details.)

With rising medical costs, insurance has become a necessity. But how much and what kind of insurance is needed? Insurance needs should be reviewed every few years with a reliable insurance agent.

Basically an older person needs two types of insurance—life and health:

1. *Life insurance.* The policy should at least cover the cost of a funeral and other cash needs in the event of death.

2. *Private health insurance.* Not all senior citizens or medical problems are covered by Medicare or Medicaid. Those who are not eligible or who receive Medicare only will need private health insurance for complete coverage or to fill the gaps not covered by these programs. "Medi-gap" or supplemental policies fill the gap left by Medicare or Medicaid.

Your insurance agent can fill you in on the types of policies best suited to the elderly. Also, you may want to check with a senior or retired citizen's program to find which insurance policies they recommend.

In Washington State, through the RSVP (Retired Senior Volunteer Program) and the Insurance Commissioner, seniors may contact S.H.I.B.A. (Senior Health Insurance Benefit Advisors). These volunteer advisors answer insurance questions, review policies, and offer teaching programs that focus on medical insurance, consumer protection, and related subjects. S.H.I.B.A. resource people work as advocates for seniors. They do not sell or solicit insurance.

For similar services (names will vary from state to state), contact the Insurance Commissioner's office at your state capital. If they are not familiar with an insurance advisory program, try several area agencies on aging. If still you are unable to untangle the bureaucratic maze, write for information to: Washington State Insurance Commissioner, c/o Insurance Building, Olympia, Wash. 98504.

Review your parent's current policy and replace or update if necessary. Here are some pitfalls to avoid in choosing a health insurance policy to cover an aging parent.

1. Be careful about obtaining a policy with a *preexisting illness exclusion*. This means that if you have and are being treated for a particular illness, the policy will not cover you if you need medical attention for that problem for a defined period of time. Many policies stipulate a three-month exclusion, some six months, and some longer. While a three-month exclusion may be satisfactory, policies with no preexisting illness exclusions would be preferable.
2. Beware of policies that advertise, "No medical examination required." These usually have a long preexisting condition exclusion. They not only don't examine the policyholder, they may not pay either.
3. Don't trust a policy simply because it was recommended by a friend or a reputable organization. Check out the terms of the policy and whether or not it meets your parent's needs.
4. Most likely, you will only need one health insurance policy. Look with suspicion on an agent who tries to sell you more than you need.
5. Some insurance policies cover home health care and skilled nursing home expenses, but few, if any, cover intermediate or custodial care.
6. Beware the policy that sets a low limit on the total number of days for hospital coverage or amount paid per year, or that excludes payment for the first few days of hospitalization. Sometimes the monthly payments promised may seem impressive, but when you actually consider hospital costs and the average length of stay you find it covers you about as adequately as a fig leaf.
7. Don't purchase a policy that permits the insurance company to

cancel if claims are too high. Your parent should have the right to renew the policy each year.

8. Be wary of "limited offers." It isn't necessary to rush into any insurance policy. If it's here today and gone tomorrow, you know it wasn't for you anyway. However, time limits based on age may be legitimate.

9. Most reputable firms allow the consumer a ten- to thirty-day period to examine an insurance policy. If, before the end of that trial period, you decide not to take it, the money must be refunded. Make certain this trial period is available.

10. Premium payments should be made by check or money order so you have a receipt. Never pay cash and never make the check out to the agent—only to the insurance company.

Major Medical policies may be an option. Unfortunately, most Major Medical policies don't insure persons over sixty-five if they are applying for the first time.

Another option to consider are the HMO's or Health Maintenance Organizations. These organizations provide insurance as well as medical coverage. Major HMO's include Kaiser-Permanente Medical Plan and Health Insurance Plan of New York (HIP).

A recent article in "Pulse," published for Kaiser-Permanente of Oregon personnel, reports that HMO's and PPO's (Preferred Provider Organizations) may be the wave of the future. The health care industry is becoming highly competitive. That's good news for us consumers, because we should be able to get good health care at reasonable costs. Why is there competition?

For one thing, there has been an increase in the number of doctors. A government report predicts over 70,000 surplus physicians by 1990. Second, more and more people are having to buy their own insurance and will be looking for the best deal. Third, the government has put stiffer regulations in the Medicare/Medicaid programs.

According to an article in *Newsweek*, April 9, 1984, "The party's over for 75% of American workers whose companies cover their medical costs. You'll be paying more of the bill yourself.

"And the party's over for hospitals and doctors who, until recently, have pretty much been able to raise fees at will. Since 1983 the federal government has been fixing the prices it pays for treating Medicare patients. In the private sector, the big corporations, labor unions, and insurance companies are forming coalitions—around 150 of them so far—to fight the runaway cost of medical treatment. . . . Business's new determination to cut the cost of health insurance claims is changing the way you receive and pay for medical care."

If you have the option of joining a HMO or PPO in your area, you may want to consider it. We recently had the opportunity to bring my mother and mother-in-law into the Kaiser Permanente HMO plan. Although monthly payments run high, about $100 for an individual to $240 for a family of four, including dental, for us the benefits have outweighed the cost. My mother, for example, was paying out more for doctor visits and prescriptions than what her monthly premiums run. Now, for each prescription, treatment, and doctor visit, she pays only $1. If she should need hospitalization, the cost would be minimal.

For older people, whose health care needs will probably increase, HMO's could be the answer. If you're interested in looking into HMO's, you may want to read an article I came across in the August 1987 *Reader's Digest* called "Should You Join an HMO?" by Donald and Diana Stroetzel (page 91).

Regardless of the type of private insurance, good coverage will probably cost plenty. Yet it is essential. I've heard horror stories about elderly people who have lost their entire savings and were forced to go on welfare because medical bills from a chronic illness or disability were not sufficiently covered by their insurance.

For those who qualify, Medicare and/or Medicaid can help take the sting out of medical costs for the elderly.

No, Medicare and Medicaid are not the same. Let's take a look at the differences.

Medicare

What is Medicare? It's a limited federal convalescent health insurance program for people sixty-five or older. Medicare is composed of two parts—Part A, hospital insurance, and Part B, medical insurance. Information about Medicare can be obtained through your Social Security office. Since it is a federal program, rules are the same throughout the United States.

Funding for the Medicare program comes through the Social Security payroll tax deductions, through premium payments of subscribers, and from the federal government's general revenues.

Who is eligible?   People sixty-five or older who qualify for Social Security or Railroad Retirement Benefits are automatically eligible. In addition, those under sixty-five who have received Supplemental Security Income (SSI), due to a disability, for at least twenty-four months, and those who require kidney dialysis, are eligible for the Part A hospital insurance program without paying a premium. Others over sixty-five can obtain benefits by paying a monthly premium.

Part B, the medical insurance program, is available to all persons over sixty-five for a monthly premium.

What services are covered?   Basically, a hospital stay, in a semiprivate room (2–4 beds); meals (special diets included); regular nursing services; rehabilitation services; drugs furnished by the facility during hospital stay; medical supplies (splints or casts); and appliances such as a wheelchair.

Medicare does not cover personal items such as television or radio, private duty nurses, or extra charges for a private room.

Part B medical insurance will pay 80 percent of what it calls "reasonable" charges for some doctor costs, outpatient hospital care, lab work, supplies, home health care, and therapy. It does not pay for routine physicals and tests, routine foot care, eye or hearing exams or eyeglasses or hearing aids, or immunizations.

Medicare benefits for nursing home residents are very limited (only about 1 percent of monies paid to nursing homes comes from Medicare).

You can apply for and learn more about Medicare by calling the Social Security office in your area.

Medicaid

Medicaid is a cooperative federal–state assistance program that provides health care services to low income and "needy" people. Medicaid services are limited to the aged with low incomes and limited assets, the blind, disabled, and others who receive public assistance.

Since the program is run by the state health or welfare agency under the general guidelines of the federal government, income guidelines and rules vary from state to state.

Medicaid does pay for nursing home care, in certified homes and for qualified patients. The nursing home personnel, the Department of Welfare, the Department of Health, or the Department of Human Resources should all be able to help you find information about and show you how to apply for Medicaid.

I might mention here that although Medicaid is essentially a public assistance program available through the welfare agency, money comes from our tax dollars. Don't be ashamed to apply for it or to help your aging parent apply for this assistance if he or she is eligible.

In addition to the Medicare and Medicaid programs, you will also want to look into whether or not your parent is eligible for SSI (Supplemental Security Income) through the Social Security Administration. And don't forget the veterans' programs for those who qualify. The Veterans Administration provides short- and long-term care to veterans.

It seems the rules are perpetually changing where the government programs are concerned and it's hard to keep up. In my research, I came across an excellent book called *Sourcebook for Older Americans* by Joseph L. Matthews. The book covers all the latest information regarding Social Security, income, rights, and benefits for older people. (Nolo Press updates the book regularly and keeps readers posted about changes in a quarterly newspaper. See page 178 for more information and the address.) If you're wandering through the bureaucratic jungle, trying to find some help for your aging parent, check this book out at your local library.

In addition to getting the proper insurance coverage and checking on your parent's eligibility for various financial assistance programs, you may want to hire an attorney to avoid some of the legal hassles that seem to run along with aging parents and their adult children.

Lawyers and Legalities

Do you have any idea how many laws there are pertaining to wills, probate, trusts, estate planning, power of attorney, guardianships, and so on in relation to aging parents? Neither do I, but I'll bet there are volumes. I can tell you what happens to me when I try to decipher or translate legal lingo. I fall asleep. It would take me years to figure out which laws pertained to me and my parent, and by that time the laws would have changed again.

How do we survive the legal system? We could hire a good lawyer. For handling details of wills, guardianships, and other such legalities, you will want a lawyer who specializes in those problems. (Whoops, we better say *attorney* because that's how they're listed in the Yellow Pages.)

Check the phone book. Generally the attorney's specialties will be listed under the name of the law firm. Sometimes, in larger cities, you will find specialty subheadings with the attorney's name under that heading. Rather than choose an attorney from the phone book, you might want to check with friends about someone they've used and been satisfied with. If you choose at random, write down several names.

Call and inquire as to the attorney's experience, expertise, and fees. Talk to a secretary, on this initial query; lawyers are notorious for charging per minute, even if it's only to tell you how great they are.

Once you and your parent have settled on a lawyer, here are some concerns that should be dealt with.

Wills

First on the legal docket for the day is wills.

A lot of people would rather not talk about wills, because discussing a will means talking about what happens when they die. Encourage your parent to have a will made up, if he or she hasn't already done so. It can save lengthy legal tie-ups in probate and prevent legal battles among family members.

A will, after all, is simply making sure your parent's desires, rather than the state's, are accomplished in regard to his or her estate. If your parent seems hesitant or you aren't certain how to broach the subject, talk about having drawn up your own will. You *have* drawn up your own will . . . haven't you?

Unfortunately, when a person dies, especially if he or she leaves a substantial estate, the family emerges from the woodwork, with "greed" oozing out of every pore. I've seen families split over who deserves what and why. A will can bypass many of those problems, but probably not all of them. The "Mom always did like you best" pouter is seldom satisfied that the will really dictates the parent's wishes.

If a will has not been made, and your parent is mentally able to do so, contact a lawyer and set up an appointment. When the will has been made, you should know:

- where the will is kept
- when, where, and by whom it was drawn up
- the attorney's name if applicable
- the name of the executor (the person who carries out the provisions of the will)
- if there is an additional letter of instruction for the disposition of personal items, such as heirlooms, furniture, jewelry—things not specifically mentioned in the will—and where it is

There is yet another problem in this area of wills. Often our parents feel strongly about leaving their children an estate. Some elderly people have actually lived in poverty so they could leave their children a little nest egg. Be aware of your parents' finances if possible and encourage them to use the money they have to cover their own living expenses.

With the will done, there should be no problem about what happens to the estate after death. However, some further steps should be taken to protect your parents' finances and see that they are properly managed now.

When a parent is disabled or handicapped, he or she may ask that you take care of the finances. In that case the best course of action is to seek legal advice as to whether you should be given *power of attorney*, made *trustee*, or become joint owner over your parent's affairs.

To save you time and money in consultation fees, it will help to know a little about these various options before you seek legal advice.

Power of Attorney

This simply means that your parent would give you the power to conduct business in his or her behalf. This power can be limited to a one-time project, such as selling a house or handling a bank account, or can be a general power of attorney that would give unlimited control over all aspects of your parent's affairs.

While standard power-of-attorney forms can be purchased at a stationery store, for your own protection and that of your parent, it might be wise to have an attorney draw up the document. That way, proper clauses dealing with your specific circumstances can be included. For example, in many states the power of attorney could be revoked if the parent became legally incapacitated. And yet incapacitation is one of the reasons for doing it in the first place. To avoid this legal hassle, the clause, "this power shall not be affected by my disability," may be inserted. (Laws vary from state to state on these amendments.)

You can only be given power of attorney if the person offering it to you has the mental capacity to understand what he is doing and signs a document witnessed by two persons besides yourself.

Joint Ownership

In joint ownership you allow someone else part ownership. Sometimes joint ownership is used to manage a parent's checking account. For example, if Mom becomes ill or is away from home, you could pay bills and deposit checks.

However, a lot of problems can develop in a joint ownership situation. For example, placing another person's name as joint owner may obligate them to federal estate and/or gift tax. Even though joint ownership may seem a simple way of helping to manage your parent's affairs, it's tricky. Make certain you are aware of all the legal potholes in that one.

Trusts

A trust is usually drawn up to turn investment securities or properties over to a trusted individual called a trustee. The trustee must follow the instructions of the trust. Properties or investments placed in trust are put on hold and remain protected until a designated time or until the parent dies, then are dispersed as the trust designates. Usually trusts are not set up unless the properties involve assets of

$50,000 to $100,000 or more. Trusts can be drawn by a parent only if he or she is mentally alert and capable.

All of these legal procedures are not without complications and cost, but one or some should be considered—before it's too late.

Guardianship

If time has slipped away and you find yourself with a parent who has become too impaired because of illness, disability, or mental deterioration to handle financial affairs, someone, perhaps you, may be appointed guardian or conservator.

This involves the painful process of having the courts declare your parent incompetent. At this last stage, we often hear the adult children cry, "Why didn't I do something sooner?"

Something probably should have been done sooner, but, because of neglect, denial, or resistance from the parent or the adult child, time has run out. Has this happened to you? Are you asking, "What now?"

Having a parent declared incompetent may be the most painful process you've ever undergone in your life. But, if the parent can no longer maintain responsibility for his or her care or financial matters, a guardianship needs to be declared.

Once it's done, it's easy to beat yourself into a mental mess wondering, *Did I do the right thing?* Punishing yourself doesn't help.

What About a Stubborn Parent?

Obviously, having a person declared incompetent in order to gain control of his or her finances should be a final resort. The best way to avoid the situation is to come to a solution beforehand. "But," you may be asking, "what about a stubborn parent?"

Mona's father insisted there was no reason for her to be concerned and stated emphatically, "I've been managing this family's finances since before you were born and I'm not going to stop now."

"But, Pop," Mona reasoned, "what if something happened to you?"

"Then you can bury me. Till then I run my own affairs."

No amount of persuasion could convince Pop to change his mind. Let's face it, some older people refuse to accept their limitations. It's understandable, but can be extremely frustrating—especially when their health is involved.

When reasoning fails, what can you do? Not much. You can't force someone to name you power of attorney or trustee. If a parent refuses to listen to the "kids," maybe someone outside the family can help. Is there a clergyman, doctor, or a friend the parent trusts enough to listen to? Maybe it's worth a try.

Above all, pray. Your prayers may not change your parent's mind, but they will give you strength, especially if you come to the place where you're forced to step in and take control.

When Do You Step In?

When and *if* can be very powerful words. Can a person know for certain when and if they should make the decision to take over? Randy's parents lived alone and seemed to be doing well; but within the last year his mother had gone almost completely blind. Since Mother had always done the bookkeeping, Randy worried about whether or not Dad could handle the added responsibility.

"Of course I can," Dad reassured his son.

However, several months later, Randy received a call from his mother.

"I just got a call from Sears," she said. They told me nothing had been paid on the account since last summer. We owe over two thousand dollars. I don't understand what's going on. When I ask, your dad tells me everything has been taken care of."

When Randy checked through his parents' desk, he found stacks of unpaid bills, and six months' worth of unopened check statements. In addition Randy discovered Dad had made some extravagant purchases. When confronted, Randy's father denied any difficulty. He became angry and ordered Randy from his home. A few hours later, Randy was sitting next to his mother's hospital bed. She'd been admitted with a fractured collarbone.

"I've never seen him so upset," she sobbed. "He threw me against the wall and kept yelling, 'I can do it myself!' What's wrong with him, Randy?"

A doctor's examination confirmed a suspected diagnosis of senile dementia.

With his parents' finances out of control, because of his father's inability to manage them and the mounting medical expenses, Randy finally gave his father an ultimatum: "Mother's moving in with us. If you want to stay with her, you'd better come too."

He did.

With legal assistance and his mother's backing, Randy was able to supervise his parents' financial affairs. His father's stubbornness (probably due, at least in part, to his dementia) caused financial loss for both Randy and his parents and a lot of grief.

Randy is not alone in facing this sort of dilemma. An article in *Business Week* stated, "next to bringing up teenagers and financing their college education, the hardest family problem faced by executives over the age of 35 is caring for their elderly parents."

In Randy's parents' case intervention was clearly indicated. The situation had become dangerous. To allow his parents continued independence, both residential and financial, would have been unsafe for them.

Other cases are not so clear-cut. I recently read an article about an older woman whose family thought her to be senile. She had been acting strange. Going for walks at all hours of the day, and hiding large amounts of money around the house.

The daughter learned after some detective work that the old woman had found $10,000 in a mattress, where her late husband had hidden it. The woman, rather than keep the money for herself, would often slip a thousand-dollar bill into the pocket of her gray overcoat, and on her walk would give the money away. Before they discovered her secret she had given away thousands of dollars to the destitute people of the city.

Was the woman eccentric? Incompetent? Some might think so. Others called her an angel.

Why am I telling you this? I think we all need to be careful that we don't misjudge an older person's actions as incompetent simply because they do what they want and what they feel is right, at times ignoring the "sensible advice" offered by their offspring.

Is There Gold in Them Thar Years?

Finances in the "golden years" is a major topic of concern. For many elderly people the question is, "I've come to my golden years now where's the gold?" Others want to know how to invest and to protect their holdings.

Many of our parents planned on living on their Social Security checks when they retired. Consequently, they felt no additional retirement programs or pension plans were necessary. Although some were able to claim meager savings, for the most part, they were counting on Social Security. For many who had lived through the depression, the retirement amount seemed adequate. With the nightmare of inflation, came the reality. The *security* in Social Security had vanished.

So what do these people do now? With no savings and their small monthly SS checks, how can they survive?

Supplemental Income for the Elderly

If your parents are sixty-five or over, or disabled, with limited income and assets, they may be eligible for SSI (Supplemental Security Income). Even though applications for SSI are usually made at the Social Security office, the two programs are not related. SSI is a joint federal–state program that was set up to provide a guaranteed minimum income level for the elderly, blind, and disabled. Eligibility is based on financial need. The basic requirements are as follows:

- Your parent must be either 65 or older, blind, or disabled.
- Their monthly income must be below a minimum amount which is established separately by each state.
- Their assets must be worth less than $1,500 (single), $2,250 (couple). Their home and car, and certain other items, are not counted or may be excluded from this amount.

There are numerous other rules and regulations. Your local Social Security office can supply you with any additional information you need.

Other means of deriving a supplemental income in elder years include:

- Your parent can execute freedom of choice in not retiring, or develop a business using his or her skills and talents.
- Encourage your parent to earn extra income by using their creative skills such as art and craft work, woodwork.
- Your parent can consider converting home equity into retirement income through "home equity conversion." This plan is not for everyone but it may be worth considering if your parents own their own home and have substantial equity in it. For more information turn back to page 59.

Another way for aging parents to make extra money or at least protect the money they have is to invest and spend wisely.

Investments in the Golden Years

Most financial advisers agree that the retirement years are not the time for highly speculative investing. High-risk investments are better made when a person is younger and more able to recoup the funds if the investment turns out to be a loss.

The aged have been especially susceptible to fraudulent activity. Fortunately, many scams are uncovered and exposed on television and newspapers. Still many elderly people suffer at the hands of con artists. Alert your parents to this danger.

For "golden years" investing, the safest and surest investments are probably in Money Markets or Certificates of Deposit. These tie up money for short periods of time (around six months) and are fairly liquid—easy to get to—in case money is needed for an emergency.

Annuities have been popular among the elderly population. At retirement or before a lump sum is invested in an annuity and while interest is earned, it is not significant. The idea here is instead of having a large amount of money to spend at one time, you have a set monthly income over a period of time, which you designate—usually ten to twenty years. Annuities can be set up through a mutual fund representative, a financial counselor, or an insurance company.

Ideally your parent will have invested in an IRA or Keogh account.

Since these are relatively new, they may not have been able to do so, or perhaps only a small amount was placed in that account. You, however, can still set up yours. If Social Security isn't so secure now, don't expect it to get better in a few years. If you haven't done so, I suggest you look into investing in an IRA or Keogh plan now.

In addition to investing, it's important to protect that income with wise money management. Fortunately, in the last few years, retired citizens have been getting discounts on practically everything from health club memberships to a steak dinner. There are unlimited ways in which older people can reduce expenditures and make it possible to live within their budgets and still have some fun.

Wise budgeting and record keeping are important for all of us, but especially for those living on fixed incomes as most older people are. They'll want to get the most out of their money. For tips on saving money on almost everything and for unique and creative ways to save, earn, and invest you'll want to study my book *From Money Mess to Money Management.*

With wise planning, investing, and spending, those older years *can* be golden years.

Funeral Arrangements

Just as wills and finances should be discussed so should funeral arrangements. Again, while some parents may want to discuss plans for their funeral, others will refuse to talk about it. You may want to use the tactic of discussing your own.

When my father died and we went in to choose a casket and make arrangements for his funeral, I had the feeling he would have preferred, like myself, to be buried in a simple pine box—no frills, no extravagant, expensive, satin-lined caskets. Unfortunately, he hadn't told us, and it was too late to ask.

As we stepped into the elegantly designed casket room, my pine box idea vanished into a gnawing guilt—*Doesn't your father deserve better?* After all, you only die once, right? We tried not to be overcome by all the elaborate trappings, but the funeral still ended up costing over $1,000. I understand we did well; the average amount spent on a funeral in America comes to around $2,400.

It is important to know the desires of your loved one—before death comes. My friend Angela tells this story:

"When Mother went back to Kansas City last month, to clean out Grandmother's apartment, she found an unworn, brand-new, white frilly dress wrapped in cellophane. The dress had been hanging on Grandmother's bedroom door. No note expressed it, but Mother surmised it was Grandma's burial dress. Gran had information about a plot scribbled on some papers in her dresser. It's sad. No one knew what she really wanted.

"I guess the ultimate in organization is to plan one's own funeral. Maybe I listen to KPDQ too much. Art Linkletter is always popping on to explain the benefits of prefuneral arrangements."

Sadly, many funeral home directors take advantage of a family's grief to make their fortune. Don't get me wrong, I have a good friend who is a funeral director. He helped us get through my dad's death beautifully; so I know some can be trusted. Unfortunately, some can't and often the family's grief is compounded by enormous funeral expenses.

Knowing your facts about funerals can help prevent problems in this area. Margaret Engel of the *Washington Post* shares some common myths about funerals:

- *Bodies have to be embalmed for health or sanitation reasons.* There is no requirement that bodies be embalmed, except in rare cases such as long delays before burial. For delays of a few days, refrigeration can be used. Embalming is not always required if a body is being shipped.
- *Embalming preserves bodies from decay.* Embalming does not have long-term effects, but only keeps a body from decomposing for about 10 days or less.
- *Heavy, sealer-type caskets preserve bodies for a long time.* No caskets, even airtight ones, preserve the body or prevent decomposition.
- *Caskets are required for all deaths, even if a body will be cremated.* Caskets are not required by law for a body that will be cremated, but some funeral homes and crematories have a policy of requiring some type of container.
- *Funeral merchandise can only be bought, not rented.*

Most funeral homes will allow you to rent a casket for visitation purposes and then sell you a cheaper version for burial.

• *Burial vaults or grave liners are required by law.* No laws require caskets to have an outer container for burial, but some cemeteries and funeral homes have policies requiring them.

Knowing what to do regarding the death of a loved one before the time comes can save much time, added grief, and even money.

Prearrangements should be made with a funeral director if your parent is expected to die at home. When the death occurs, your only responsibility will be to call the funeral director. He or she will give you any necessary instructions and will see that the body is properly cared for.

If the death is unexpected, the physician and possibly the county coroner will have to be called in.

These instructions may vary from state to state, but to save yourself worry and unnecessary burdens, I recommend prearrangements with the funeral home.

As we close the door on finances and legalities regarding our parents, we open another door into the final frontier for our aging parent—death. Here we'll explore feelings of fear and denial, discover how to celebrate life from beginning to end, and learn how to say good-bye.

13

Aging: The Final Frontier

The statistics on death are quite impressive, one out of one people die.

GEORGE BERNARD SHAW

Facing the Inevitable

In our plans to help our aging parents, one of the inevitable problems we will face is death. These final stages are probably the most important.

Before we can accept death for our aging parents, we must first accept death for ourselves. We must learn how to talk about death and to communicate in a helpful way to the dying. We must also learn how to grieve so that we grow through the process and are not overcome by it. It is even possible to come to the point where we feel comfortable about death.

We all know deep down that we can't stop death or even change the process. Even though we can't stop death, we can have some control over the final outcome. In the next few pages, I've outlined a plan for celebrating life. The first part of that plan is to understand death.

Understanding Death

Death is the end of life—as we know it.

For me, death means embarking on a new and adventurous frontier.

159

My faith promises me life after death. Since I've never died, I can't give you a blow-by-blow account of what happens in the last chapter. All I know is, in my Book—the Bible—those of us who believe in the Lord will experience a happy ending.

I've tried looking at death from different perspectives and found that no matter where I turned, no one could offer me hope. Looking at death was scary and depressing. As a nursing student, my classmates and I studied death and dying and, of course, learned of the afterdeath experiences written about by Elisabeth Kübler-Ross. Her accounts seemed to verify that life indeed went on after the body gave up its ghost.

Her works confirmed my faith in a supreme being—God. Consequently, I have come to depend on God to carry me safely through death into His perfect world beyond this life.

Some people have made comments like, "Trust in God? That's for people who are too weak to make it on their own strength."

That may be true, but I'll match my strength in God against people power any day. I've never met a crisis I couldn't cope with, and I have no fear of death because I really believe God is with me.

I'm certain most of you have heard or read these words from the Twenty-third Psalm, "The Lord is my Shepherd. . . . Even though I walk through the valley of the shadow of death, I fear no evil; for thou art with me. . . ."

The Bible offers many verses that encourage and promise us that we will live forever:

> For God so loved the world that he gave his only Son, that whoever believes in him should not perish but have eternal life. For God sent the Son into the world, not to condemn the world, but that the world might be saved through him (John 3:16, 17).
> . . . Death is swallowed up in victory. O death, where is thy victory? O death, where is thy sting? (1 Corinthians 15:54, 55.)

With these promises and the knowledge that when my life on earth ends, I'll be moving in with God—how could I be afraid of death? Even though I could accept death and not be afraid for myself, there was still this business of being able to talk to people who were actually dying. As a nurse I had to, but I fought any personal contact. I just didn't know what to say.

What Do You Say to a Dying Man?

I'm ashamed to admit it, but for a long time I tried to stay away from the patients who were dying. Eventually I came to understand the needs of terminally ill patients and I tried to meet those needs. I'll never forget the first time I actually helped a dying man.

As I stopped at Tom's bed during rounds, he seemed restless. "Are you okay?" I asked.

"Would you be?" he challenged.

"Probably not. Do you need something for pain?"

He nodded.

"I'll be back as soon as I can." I finished my rounds and hurried to the nurses' station to draw up his pain medication. My mind and stomach churned as I wondered, *What if Tom wants to talk to me?*

"God," I offered up my plea for help. "What do you say to a dying man who's only forty-nine?"

Don't be a dummy, I said to myself. *He's hurting; all he wants is something to ease the pain.*

But after I'd given Tom the injection he said, "Could you sit here awhile? I won't be able to sleep and I could use some company. Dying gets sorta lonely."

I swallowed hard barely able to blink back the tears. Then with learned composure I replied, "Sure," and pulled an armchair close to the bed.

"You drew night shift this week." It was more a statement than a question.

I nodded.

"Oh—" his voice broke. "I'm gonna die. I don't mind so much for myself—yes, I do. But my wife and kids. What are they going to do without me?"

I couldn't answer him. I never could talk and cry at the same time. But he didn't seem to notice. I touched his shoulder to comfort him. He reached up, took my hand in his and held it there. He talked and cried, for about an hour. I just sat there and cried with him. Finally, he let go of my hand and said, "Thanks for staying. You helped me a lot."

"But," I stammered, "I didn't say anything."

"You listened."

I had listened. Not because I wanted to, but because I didn't have a choice. Sometimes I have to thank God for the craziest things. That night I thanked Him for making me cry so hard I couldn't talk. What a lesson. Sometimes the best counsel you can give is to shut up and listen.

From that time on I developed a sensitive spirit toward the dying. I tried not to think of my comfort, but of theirs. My lessons didn't stop there. Each time I cared for a dying patient, God showed me how life and death are all wrapped up in the pattern of nature He created.

I learned to face the inevitable, to look on death as the final frontier. A new and exciting journey, that brings us closer to God.

Sometimes though, the journeys seemed agonizing. Especially those first few I took with small children. In anger I shook my fist at God and cried, "Why? They're so young." I still ask why sometimes, though no longer in anger. Somehow, through all the tragedy, it is enough to know God is in control—no matter what.

You never get used to death—not if you remain sensitive to others' needs. Oh, I've seen some who act used to it, but mostly they've covered their hearts with callouses made from denial so it doesn't hurt them anymore. I never wanted callouses. A long time ago, I prayed that God would always leave me open and vulnerable to the hurts and needs of others. He has.

Everybody needs somebody to talk to. The dying especially need a friend to confide in—someone who understands. They need a friend with whom they can share their deepest fear, sorrow, and joy. They need to talk about it.

Talk About It

I'm not alone in my beliefs. Most of the experts on death and dying share the same thoughts.

Yet, talking it over is sometimes the hardest part. We often think, *If I don't talk about it, maybe it will go away.* But death doesn't go away. It just slips in like a silent enemy and steals away the people we love.

Some of you may never be able to talk about death or talk to your dying parent without feeling the need to say, "Let's not talk about it just now."

It's okay to feel that way, just don't say it. If you can't talk, then be quiet and listen. If you have to cry, then cry. That's okay too. In fact, it's more than okay. Nothing shows the compassion of how much you really care more than tears.

On the other hand there are some people who will be gifted in the area of listening to and talking with those who are dying. It's important to encourage these individuals, even if you want to protect them—even if they are children. In this next story you'll see why.

Helping Gram Die

"Ben, I don't think it's good for a girl Susan's age to be spending so much time with Gram. Susan should be out enjoying life."

"She loves her grandmother, Tess," Ben replied. "We ought to be happy she's willing to help us take care of her. Most kids would be griping about us 'ruining their lives.' Susan's different since Gram came home. She doesn't seem so selfish anymore. And you've got to admit, she's developed the patience of a saint."

"That's just it, twelve-year-olds don't sit for hours reading to a grandparent. The other day I overheard Gram talking about dying. Of course I hurried in and changed the subject."

"It's good for Gram to talk about it. The nurse told us talking it through makes it easier for all of us."

"I can't. And Susan's too young. I don't want her to see Gram die." Tess turned and buried her face in her husband's shoulder.

"It's okay, Honey," Ben smoothed his wife's hair. "I'll talk to Susan. Only you'll have to stop the waterworks. I'd rather not have you launder my shirt while I'm wearing it."

"I'm sorry," Tess sniffed and mopped her face with the Kleenex he'd handed her.

Ben found his daughter, as he suspected, curled up in a chair beside Gram's bed. Hand in hand, they'd fallen asleep. He surveyed the spectrum of life that greeted him. Susan just beginning; Gram coming to the end. He stared unseeing at the scene before him, trying to make some sense of it. How could he tell the girl to stop doing what was so obviously right? As if she sensed his presence, Susan stirred, opened her eyes, and smiled.

She gently removed her hand from the old woman's grasp, placed her finger to her pursed lips in a gesture of silence, and tiptoed from the room.

"Did you want to see me, Dad?" Susan whispered.

Ben nodded. "Sit down, Suzie, we need to talk a minute. Honey," he paused. "Your Mom's been worried about you. She thinks maybe you've been spending too much time with Gram."

"Am I making Gram too tired?" Susan asked.

"No, Honey, it's just . . . well, wouldn't you rather be out playing with your friends? You've been neglecting them lately."

"Oh, Daddy," Susan sighed. "They'll understand. I'll have plenty of time to play with them later."

"I'm not sure I understand."

Susan chewed her lower lip. Finally, she stood and knelt at her father's side. "Daddy, Gram needs me to help her die."

"But Suzie, there's your mom and me . . ." even as he spoke, Ben knew his little girl was right. He remembered the Scripture verse Matthew 19:14. He pictured the disciples shooing away the children and heard Jesus' words, "Let the children come to me, and do not hinder them; for to such belongs the kingdom of heaven."

"Daddy," Susan placed her hand in his. "You still don't understand. Mom takes care of Gram, but she's afraid to talk to her about what's wrong. It hurts her too much to stay and listen to Gram talk about the cancer and what it feels like to die. You help take care of Gram too, but not enough 'cause you're at work.

"Gram says it's like I'm walkin' her clear to the gates of heaven. And I promised to be there when she says good-bye. I'm giving Gram a present, Daddy. And it's something she can't get from anyone but me."

Learn From the Children

It has always amazed me that children, those little ones we try to protect from the ugly realities of life, are the ones who seem to understand and react most naturally to death. Perhaps it's because the older we get, the closer we come to death ourselves. And rather than face it, we turn away whenever it comes near. We can learn from children when it comes to responding to death and grief.

I recently read yet another story that shows how natural the child's understanding can be of the life and death process. In the book *Grief*, Haddon W. Robinson writes, "A little girl lost a playmate in death, and one day reported to her family that she had gone to comfort the sorrowing mother.

" 'What did you say?' the father asked.

" 'Nothing,' the child replied. 'I just climbed up on her lap and cried with her.' "

It seems that somewhere between childhood and becoming grown-up, we lose much of our spontaneous sensitivity. We don't want death to happen. We keep wanting to protect ourselves and others from it. We can fight, deny, run, but death won't be stopped by any of us.

Comes the Sorrow

Trying to stop death is like holding back the night. Like night death comes. And with the darkness, sure and swift, comes the sorrow. After sorrow we can experience joy in the hope of the morning light.

You will notice that I placed an order in this sequence. First death and sorrow, then joy.

A great deal has been written about death, dying, and the grieving process over the last few years, but suffering certainly is nothing new. Many of us have lost the art of being sorrowful. Having been taught to stifle ourselves, we have to learn all over again that it's okay to cry.

I found in my studies, that the people of biblical times handled sorrow best. These people didn't suppress their sorrow. In fact, sorrow or mourning was included as an important part of the dying. In 2 Samuel 1:11, 12, we read, "Then David took hold of his clothes, and rent them; and so did all the men who were with him; and they mourned and wept and fasted until evening for Saul and for Jonathan his son and for the people of the Lord and for the house of Israel because they had fallen by the sword." We could learn a thing or two from the "old ways."

So many times, we shove aside our grief and sorrow, thinking we don't have time or, *Big boys (girls) don't cry*. Other people tranquilize their sorrow by taking drugs to dull the pain. But these measures don't eliminate the hurt, they only prolong it.

I believe it is essential that the whole process of sorrow, from the anger, denial, guilt, and emptiness, to the acceptance and the wellness, be allowed to happen naturally.

If sorrow can't be released, the grief builds inside us. We can be certain that the sorrow will be released one way or another. If not under our control, then without control. In unleashed anger, bitterness, resentment—somehow, the body will have its way. How much better to let sorrow happen naturally.

It is only through this process that we can learn to accept death and feel the joy of life again.

Knowing about the process ahead of time makes it much easier to bear. When my grandmother died, I had already learned to accept death. I knew about grieving. Even so, grief filled me like lead. Its weight burdened me for days. Then, finally, the tears subsided and the weight fell away. I could actually delight in the joy of her release from the earth and her homecoming in heaven.

Sometimes the joy we should eventually come into is shrouded in a heavy curtain of guilt from a broken relationship that was never resolved. Make your peace with your parents before the end comes.

> Death ends a life ... but it does not end a relationship which struggles on in the survivor's mind ... toward some resolution which it never finds.
>
> ROBERT ANDERSON
> *I Never Sang for My Father*

Our youth pastor shares this very special story to illustrate the importance of saying, "I love you," before it's too late.

"Mrs. Stender lived three houses down the block. She was the most loving woman I've ever known—a silver-haired grandma in her calico-print dresses, heavy nylon stockings, and big thick black 'grandma shoes.'

"All during my growing up years in Bismarck, North Dakota, her home was always open to me. She had just the sort of home you'd expect a grandma to have—with a big mantel clock and a cuckoo clock which she let my brother or me set every day. She had one of those old treadle sewing machines and every day we played airplane. We'd pump that thing and imagine flying to all sorts of places we'd find in the *National Geographic.*

"A big swing sat on the porch. We would sit out on the porch for hours while she read books and told stories. She was more than the old widow lady down the block—she was a grandma, a teacher, and a friend.

"With my school just a block away from her house, I used to stop after school every night. But as I grew into junior high and high school I began thinking about other things—like girls, and sports, and girls. And I just stopped dropping by.

"Pretty soon, not intentionally, a kid kind of drops the old lady on the block. I just sort of forgot about her. But she never forgot about me. Through the years, she continued to give my brother and me presents on birthdays and Christmas and would often invite the whole family over.

"Then I went away to college and never really thought about Mrs. Stender. A few days before Valentine's Day, a friend of mine went into a Hallmark store to buy a valentine for his mom. Since I was with him, I decided to get one for my mom too. Now, you've got to understand that I just didn't go around doing this sort of thing. I was too involved with college life. So, I got the card and signed it, 'Love, Larry,' I'd done my good deed, right?

"As I was leaving the store, the thought of Mrs. Stender filled my mind. The force of the thought impressed me so much that I went back in the store and picked out a card. Then, instead of just signing it 'Love, Larry,' I found myself pouring my heart out to her. I thanked her and told her how much I loved her, how much she meant to me, and how much I appreciated her input into my life.

"As I sent the card, I thought, *This is weird.* It was probably the first time in my life I'd ever openly shared like that with another person.

"A couple of weeks later, I received a phone call from my mother. She was crying. She said, 'Larry, that's the most beautiful thing you've ever done.'

" 'What do you mean, Mom?'

"Then she said, 'Remember that letter you wrote to Mrs. Stender? Well she read the letter and called me over to read it to me. She cried

over that letter. Mrs. Stender told me how important and meaningful
it was and how good it made her feel.'

"I didn't want her to know how choked up I'd gotten and just replied, 'Oh, yeah, yeah.'

"Mom continued, 'I left Mrs. Stender a happy woman, and later on
that day they found her dead.'

"My letter was basically the last thing she had read before she died.

"Years later when I became a Christian, I knew the idea to buy that
card had come from God. Through that experience I realize how important it is to express our love, appreciation, and thankfulness to
people before they die."

We have so many unspoken feelings toward our parents and friends
and too often we don't communicate them. Then when someone we
love dies, we experience a deep sense of guilt, because we never said,
"I love you."

Talk about life—and about death.

Allow the grieving process to take its course in yourself and in
others.

Tell those older people in your life that you love and appreciate
them.

There are many helps contained in this book, with hope popping up
all over, and as for coping, well, between the help and hope, and
knowing you are not alone, plus the power of prayer, you *can* cope. I
know it.

Caring for your aging parents may be the hardest task you've ever
encountered, but it may also be the most rewarding.

Come, let us celebrate birth, and death, for life cannot be lived
without both.

Two of a Kind

Her skin wrinkled, paper thin over blue veins;
His is six-month baby smooth, honey-colored with a rosy hue.
Her hands touch him lightly;
His pull her hair.
She has some bald spots.
He does, too.
She talks in words that only he can understand.
He laughs, but she can't hear.
Two of her front teeth are missing—
  it doesn't matter,
He hasn't *any.*
Born in eighteen eighty-four,
She has almost lived a lifetime;
He has just begun.
They sit together
  spanning the century,
  each so very close
  to the Source of Life,
Two of God's children.

NANCY WHITE CARLSTROM

14

More Help and Where to Find It

This is your resource chapter. It lists articles, books, booklets, and organizations to help you find everything you always wanted to know about the various aspects of aging. The titles, names, and addresses here will provide more help as you continue to care for your aging parent(s).

Aging Awareness

Articles:

"Aging Americans." *Psychology Today,* January 1984, pp. 22–41.
"The Great Gray Years." *Guideposts,* January–October 1984.
Series of articles on aging.
Moore, Pat. "My Adventure in Old Age." *Guideposts,* January 1984, pp. 2–7.

Books:

Anderson, Margaret J. *Looking Ahead—The Realities of Aging: Face Them With Faith.* St. Louis, Mo.: Concordia Publishing House, 1978.
Brindley, Louis. *They Must Have Seen Me Coming.* New York: St. Martin's Press, 1978.
Butler, R. N. *Why Survive? Being Old in America.* New York: Harper & Row, 1975.

Calhoun, Richard B. *In Search of the New Old—Redefining Old Age in America.* New York: Elsevier, 1978.

Comfort, Alex. *A Good Age.* New York: Simon and Schuster, 1976.

Cowley, Malcolm. *The View From 80.* New York: Viking Press, 1980.

Farber, Norma. *How Does It Feel to Be Old?* New York: E.P. Dutton, 1979.

Freese, Arthur S. *The End of Senility.* New York: Arbor House, 1978.

Hale, Charlotte. *The Super Years.* Old Tappan, N.J.: Fleming H. Revell, 1983.

Maclay, Elise. *Green Winter—Celebrations of Old Age.* New York: Reader's Digest Press, 1977.

Myerhoff, Barbara. *Number Our Days.* New York: E.P. Dutton, 1979.

National Council on Aging. *Channels of Communication for Reaching Older Americans.* Washington, D.C.: National Council on Aging, 1985.

Magazines:

Aging. U.S. Department of Health and Human Services, Office of Human Development Services Administration on Aging. This magazine may be ordered from: Superintendent of Documents, Government Printing Office, Washington, D.C. 20402. (Check your local library for their reference copy.)

Aging reports on programs for, by, and with the 33 million people sixty years of age and over in the United States. It reports on activities of state area agencies and foreign countries and keeps people up to date in the field of aging.

50 Plus. Reader Service Department, P.O. Box 312, Dalton, Mass. 01226.

Mature Living, may be ordered from: Promotions Section MSN 110, 127 Ninth Avenue, North, Nashville, Tenn. 37234.

A Christian-oriented magazine to "enrich the senior years."

Mature Outlook, published bimonthly, may be ordered from: *Mature Outlook,* P.O Box 1205, Glenview, Ill. 60025.

Modern Maturity, Published bimonthly by the American Association of Retired Persons, 215 Long Beach Boulevard, Long Beach, Calif. 90801.

You may want to check these various magazines on Aging out at your local library before subscribing.

Organizations:

American Association of Retired Persons, Administrative Offices, National Headquarters, 1909 K Street NW, Washington, D.C. 20049; Western Office, 215 Long Beach Blvd., Long Beach, Calif. 90801.

AARP publishes *Modern Maturity* magazine and offers many other booklets and pamphlets on aging.

American Geriatrics Society, 10 Columbus Circle, Suite 1470, New York, N.Y. 10019.

The Society publishes a monthly journal and a newsletter.

Center for the Study of Aging, 706 Madison Avenue, Albany, N.Y. 12208.

Children of Aging Parents, 2761 Trenton Road, Levittown, Pa. 19056.

Self-help group devoted to education, support, guidance, and the development of coping skills among care-givers to the elderly. Publishes newsletter and other self-help materials.

Gerontological Society of America, 1411 K Street NW, Washington, D.C. 20005.

Gray Panthers, 311 S. Juniper Street, Suite 601, Philadelphia, Pa. 19107. (215) 545-6555.

The Panthers are advocates for senior rights, working to combat agism and age discrimination. They publish *The Network Newspaper* bimonthly.

National Association of Area Agencies on Aging, 600 Maryland Avenue SW, West Wing 208, Washington, D.C. 20024.

These agencies can help you locate information on services for the aging in your community.

National Association of Mature People, P.O. Box 26792, Oklahoma City, Okla. 73126.

They publish *Best Years* magazine bimonthly.

National Council on the Aging, 600 Maryland Avenue SW, West Wing 100, Washington, D.C. 20024.

You can order a free listing of publications on the aging.

National Council of Senior Citizens, 925 15th Street NW, Washington, D.C. 20005.

National Interfaith Coalition on Aging, P.O. Box 1924, 298 S. Hull Street, Athens, Ga. 30603.

Aging: Additional Reading

Books:

Anderson, Margaret J. *Your Aging Parents—When and How to Help.* St. Louis, Mo.: Concordia Publishing House, 1979.

Bianchi, Eugene C. *Aging as a Spiritual Journey.* New York: The Crossroad Publishing Company, 1982.

Cohen, Stephen Z. *The Other Generation Gap.* Chicago: Argus Communications, 1979.

Crichton, Jean. *The Age Care Source Book.* New York: Simon & Schuster, 1987.

Edinberg, Mark. *Talking with Your Aging.* Boston: Shambala, 1987.

Galton, Lawrence. *Don't Give Up on an Aging Parent.* New York: Crown Publishers, 1978.

Gillies, John. *A Guide to Caring for and Coping With Aging Parents.* Nashville: Thomas Nelson Publishers, 1981.

Gorsuch, Gary W. *Uncle . . . A Jerriatric Love Story.* 1983. Rt. 3, Box 292, Sherwood, Oreg. 97140.

Groseclose, Kel. *Three Speed Dad in a Ten Speed World.* Minneapolis: Bethany House, 1983.

Hayes, Helen, and Gladney, Marion G. *Our Best Years.* New York: Doubleday, 1984.

Horne, Jo. *Caregiving: Helping an Aging Loved One.* Glenview, Ill.: Scott, Foresman & Co., 1987.

Kosberg, Jordan I. *Abuse and Maltreatment of the Elderly—Causes and Interventions.* London: John Wright, PSG, Inc., 1983.

Landau, Elaine. *Growing Old in America.* New York: Messner, 1985.

Otten, June, and Shelley, Florence D. *When Your Parents Grow Old.* New York: Funk & Wagnalls, 1976.

Rossi, Ted. *Step By Step: How to Actively Insure the Best Possible Care for Your Aging Relative.* New York: Warner Books, 1987.

Silverstone, Barbara, and Hyman, Helen Kandel. *You and Your Aging Parent.* New York: Pantheon Books, 1976.

Smith, Bert Kruger. *Aging in America.* Boston: Beacon Press, 1973.

Alzheimer's Disease

Articles:

The Coordinator, January 1984. 11417 Vanowen Street, North Hollywood, Calif. 91605.
Several excellent articles and helps on Alzheimer's in this issue.
Generations. Western Gerontological Society, Fall 1982.
Issue devoted entirely to Alzheimer's disease. Contains about twenty articles for family and health care professionals.
"A Slow Death of the Mind." *Newsweek,* December 3, 1984, pp. 56–61.

Books:

Kelly, William E., M.D. *Alzheimer's Disease and Related Disorders—Research and Management.* Springfield, Ill.: Charles C Thomas, 1984.
Informative, but technical—at times difficult to understand.
Mace, Nancy L., M.A., and Peter V. Rabins, M.D. *The 36-Hour Day.* Baltimore: The Hopkins University Press, 1981.
A family guide to caring for persons with Alzheimer's disease, related dementing illnesses, and memory loss in later life.
Powell, Lenore S., Ed. D., and Courtice, Katie. *Alzheimer's Disease—a Guide for Families.* Reading, Mass.: Addison-Wesley Publishing Company, 1983.
Seymour, Claire. *Precipice—Learning to Live with Alzheimer's Disease.* New York: Vantage Press, 1983.

Booklets:

Cohen, D. and Eisdorfer, C. *Family Handbook on Alzheimer's Disease.* Health Advancement Series, 1982. Available from the Alzheimer's Disease Society, 1435 Tenth Street, Fort Lee, N.J. 07024.
Lincoln, M. *Managing the Person with Intellectual Loss (Dementia or Alzheimer's Disease) at Home.* The Burke Rehabilitation Center, 1980. Copies may be obtained from the center at 785 Mamaroneck Avenue, White Plains, N.Y. 10605.
Q & A: *Alzheimer's Disease.* National Institute of Health, Publication number 80-1646. NIH Information Office, Building 31, Room 5C-36, NIH, Bethesda, Md. 20205.
Discusses symptoms, diagnosis, efforts to learn cause, glossary of terminology.

Organizations:

Alzheimer's Disease and Related Disorders Association (ADRDA), 360 North Michigan Avenue, Suite 601, Chicago, Ill. 60601. (312) 853-3060.

This Association publishes a newsletter on research and problems of Alzheimer's patients and their families, assists in organizing family support groups, dispenses literature, and promotes public awareness of AD.

Family Survival Project, 1736 Divisadero, San Francisco, Calif. 94115. (415) 921-5400.

Contact the project for a list of local support groups or information on Alzheimer's.

Death and Dying

Books:

Bayly, Joseph. *The View From a Hearse.* Elgin, Ill.: David C. Cook, 1969.

Cameron, Jean. *For All That Has Been—Time to Live and Time to Die.* New York: Macmillan Publishing Co., Inc., 1982.

Kopp, Ruth Lewshenia, M.D., with Sorenson, Stephen. *Encounter With Terminal Illness.* Grand Rapids, Mich.: Zondervan Publishing House, 1980.

Lewis, C. S. *A Grief Observed.* New York: Seabury Press, 1961.

Robinson, Haddon W. *Grief.* Grand Rapids, Mich.: Zondervan Publishing House, 1976.

Organizations:

National Hospice Organization, 1901 N. Fort Meyer Drive, Suite 902, Arlington, Va. 22209.

Also, check with your local hospitals or physician for information on area hospice programs.

Emotional Helps for Dealing With Aging Parents

Books:

Bennett, Rita. *Emotionally Free.* Old Tappan, N.J.: Fleming H. Revell Company, 1982.

Butler, Robert N., and Lewis, Myrna I. *Aging & Mental Health.* New York: New American Library, 1983.

Lieff, Jonathan D., M.D. *Your Parent's Keeper: A Handbook of Psychiatric Care for the Elderly.* Cambridge, Mass.: Ballanger Publishing Co., 1984.

Vaswig, William L. *At Your Word, Lord.* Minneapolis: Augsburg, 1982.

Vaswig, William L. *I Prayed, He Answered.* Minneapolis: Augsburg, 1977.

Organizations:

National Support Center for Families of Aging, P.O. Box 245, Swarthmore, Pa. 19081. (215) 544-5933. Publication: "Help for Families of Aging."

Preaching & Prayer Ministries, 14401 Issaquah-Hobart Road, SE, Issaquah, Wash. 98027-8223.

This organization publishes a newsletter, "Response." Pastor W. L. Vaswig heads the organization and has done a series of tapes on faith, prayer, and healing which are available through "The Life Institute." For information on seminars, or catalog of books and tapes on prayer and healing, or more information write to the above address.

The Quickened Word, Ira Kellman Ministries, P.O. Box 35187, Tulsa, Okla. 74153.

A truly God-inspired healing and miracle ministry with spirit-filled seminars, Bible studies, and services, by evangelist and "fulfilled" Jew, Ira Kellman. Books and tapes are available and information on the ministry may be obtained by writing to the above address.

Also, check with local churches for support groups, ministries, and programs on caring for the elderly.

Video:

"Crisis or Transition," and "Conquering Negative Emotions," by DeLoss Friesen, 1983. East West Video Productions, Inc., 12345 NE 152nd Street, Brush Prairie, Wash. 98606. (206) 254-1980.

Entertainment

Books:

Brandt, Catherine. *You're Only Old Once: Devotions in Large Print.* Minneapolis: Augsburg, 1977.
Janss, Edmund W. *Making the Second Half the Best Half.* Minneapolis: Bethany House, 1984.
Merrill, Toni. *Activities for the Aged and Infirm.* Springfield, Ill.: Charles C Thomas, 1977.

Booklets:

Christ in Our Home, Large Print Edition, quarterly devotional by Augsburg Publishing House, 426 South 5th Street, Box 1209, Minneapolis, Minn. 55440.

Organizations:

Elder Craftsman, 135 E. 65th Street, New York, N.Y. 10021.
Elderhostel, 100 Boylston Street, Suite 200, Boston, Mass. 02116. Combines continuing education with travel to more than three hundred major college and university campuses.
National Institute of Senior Centers (NISC), 600 Maryland Avenue SW, West Wing 100, Washington, D.C. 20024.
Senior Citizens Centers: Listings for centers across the country are available through the National Council on the Aging and the National Council of Senior Citizens. Check with your local library or write directly to the NCOA or NCSC (see addresses on page 172).

Tapes:

American Bible Society, 1865 Broadway, New York, N.Y. 10023. For Bible studies and devotionals on tape.
"The Living Testament," in living sound from *The Living Bible*, paraphrased. Wheaton, Ill.: Tyndale House Publishers, 1973.
Lutheran Tape Ministry, Box 125, Seward, Neb. 68434
Reigner Recording Library, Union Theological Seminary, Richmond, Va. 23227. Large selection of religious tapes. Catalog available for fee.

Check your local bookstores for large print edition books and magazines, tapes, and other entertaining materials for the elderly.

Libraries: An excellent source of entertaining materials, large print books, magazines, records, tapes, video. Be sure to check church libraries for biblically based messages on casette tapes.

Financial and Legal Helps

Books:

Lammers, William W. Andrus Gerontology Center University of Southern California. *Public Policy and the Aging.* CQ Press, a division of Congressional Quarterly Inc., 1414 22nd Street NW, Washington, D.C. 20037, 1983.

Matthews, Joseph L. and Berman, Dorothy Matthews. *Sourcebook for Older Americans—Income, Rights and Benefits.* Nolo Press, 950 Parker Street, Berkeley, Calif. 94710, 1983. (Write for Update Service & Legal Directory.)

Rushford, Patricia H. *From Money Mess to Money Management.* Old Tappan, N.J.: Fleming H. Revell Company, 1984.

Booklets:

1980 Chartbook of Federal Programs in Aging, by Irma Schechter. Library of Congress #ISSN 0197-0429, 1980 Care Reports, Inc., Washington, D.C.

Your Medicare Handbook, SSA-74-10050. U.S. Department of Health and Human Services, Social Security Administration, U.S. Government Printing Office, Superintendent of Documents, Washington, D.C. 20402.

Organizations:

Legal Counsel for the Elderly, 1909 K Street NW, Washington, D.C. 20049. (202) 662-4933.

Legal services for the Elderly, 132 West 43rd Street, 3rd Floor, New York, N.Y. 10036. (212) 595-1340.

Geriatric Clothing

Fashion-Able Company, Rock Hill, New Jersey 09553

GERI-FASHIONS, 3006 SE 81st, Portland, Oreg. (503) 777-4225. Provides "lovely hand-made, nominally priced garments designed especially for nursing home residents—all with back openings."

Vocational Guidance and Rehabilitation Service, 2239 E. 55th Street, Cleveland, Ohio 44103. Write for catalog on clothing designed for the elderly and disabled.

Home Care

Articles:

Jacoby, Susan. "When a Parent Can No Longer Live Alone." *McCall's*, April 1978, pp. 118–19.

Books:

American Red Cross, *Home Nursing Textbook*. New York: Doubleday & Co., 1963.

DuFresne, Florine. *Home Care: An Alternative to the Nursing Home*. Elgin, Ill.: The Brethren Press, 1983.

Gray, Katherine V. *Caresharing: How to Relate to the Frail Elderly*. Minneapolis: Ebenezer Center for Aging & Human Development, 1984.

Hooker, Susan, MCSP. *Caring for Elderly People*. London: Routledge & Kegan Paul, 1976.

Landsberger, Betty H. *Long Term Care for the Elderly: A Comparative View of Layers of Care*. New York: St. Martin's Press, 1985.

Portnow, J., M.D. with M. Houtmann, R.N. *Home Care for the Elderly: A Complete Guide*. New York: McGraw-Hill, 1987.

Booklets:

Home Health Care Catalog. Available through your local Sears stores, or write: Home Health Care Catalog, Sears Roebuck & Co., Department 608, BSC8, 2 North La Salle, Chicago, Ill. 60612.

Johnson, Michael, R.N., M.S.W. *I'd Rather Be Home*. A practical guide for individuals, families, and professionals. Copies may be ordered from Consulting Opinion, 375 NE 163rd, Seattle, Wash. 98155.

Lincoln, M. *Managing the Person With Intellectual Loss (Dementia or Alzheimer's Disease) at Home.* The Burke Rehabilitation Center, 1980. Copies may be obtained from the center at 785 Mamaroneck Avenue, White Plains, N.Y. 10605.

National Home Caring Council. "All About Home Care: A Consumer's Guide." For copies write to the council at 235 Park Avenue South, New York, N.Y. 10003.

Organizations:

Hillhaven Home Health Services, 1120 South Robertson Boulevard, Los Angeles, Calif. 90035.

Homemakers' Home and Health Care Services, 3651 Van Rick Drive, Kalamazoo, Mich. 49001.

National Homecaring Council, 235 Park Avenue South, New York, N.Y. 10003.

National Institute on Adult Day Care, c/o National Council on Aging, 600 Maryland Avenue SW, West Wing 100, Washington, D.C. 20024. (202) 479-1200.

Staff Builders Home Health Care, Inc., Dept. M, 122 East 42nd Street, New York, N.Y. 10168.

Visiting Nurses, National League for Nursing, 10 Columbus Circle, New York, N.Y. 10019.

Housing

Articles:

"Housing Needs: The Choices Increase." *U.S. News & World Report,* Sept. 1, 1980, pp. 56–58.

"Living Independently, New Options for Older Americans," *Better Homes & Gardens,* November 1983, pp. 103–09.

Wallis, Claudia. "Day Care Centers for the Old." *Time,* Jan. 18, 1982, p. 60.

Books:

Holter, Paul. *Guide to Retirement Living.* Chicago: Rand McNally.

Musson, Noverre. *The National Directory of Retirement Residences.* New York: Frederick Fell. Check library or local bookstore.

Powell, M. Lawton and Hoover, S. L. *Community Housing: Choices for Older Americans.* New York: Springer Publishing Co., 1981.

Booklets:

✓*Continuing Care Homes, A Guidebook for Consumers.* Consumer Guidebook, American Association of Homes for the Aging, 1050 17th Street NW, Suite 770, Washington, D.C. 20036.

✓Daily, Linda. *Housing Options for the Elderly.* Editorial Research Report, Aug. 6, 1982. Congressional Quarterly, Inc. 1414 22nd Street NW, Washington, D.C. 20037.

✓*A Guide for Selection of Retirement Housing.* Published by the National Council on Aging, 1828 L Street NW, Washington, D.C. 20036.

Home Equity Conversion. National Center for Home Equity Conversion, 110 E. Main, Room 1010, Madison, Wis. 53703.

Shared Housing Resource Center, Inc., 6344 Greene Street, Philadelphia, Pa. 19144. Write for listing of shared housing opportunities and information about the concept. They publish a *Shared Housing Quarterly.*

Maintaining Independence

Books:

"Directory of Adult Day Care Centers," ed. by E. Robins, September 1980, from Health Standards and Quality Bureau, Dogwood East Building, 1849 Gwynn Oak Avenue, Baltimore, Md. 21207. Lists centers by state, with address, phone number, director, sponsoring organization, program, and daily census.

Kreisler, Jack and Nancy. *Catalog of Aids for the Disabled.* New York: McGraw-Hill Book Co., 1982.

Sargent, Jean Vieth. *An Easier Way—Handbook for the Elderly and Handicapped.* Ames: Iowa State University Press, 1981, New York: Walker and Company, 1982.

Booklets:

Communi-Care, a LIFELINE home telephone system. For information write to: Staff Builders Health Care Services, 122 East 42nd Street, New York, N.Y. 10168.

Handle Yourself With Care, Administration on Aging, Washington, D.C. 20201.

Lifeline, A Personal Emergency Response Program. Lifeline Systems, Inc., Waltham, Mass.

Preventing Crime Through Education: How to Spot a Con Artist, NRTA/AARP, 1901 K Street NW, Washington D.C. 20049.

Protection for the Elderly, Consumer Bulletin No. 9, Federal Trade Commisison, 6th and Pennsylvania Avenue NW, Washington, D.C. 20508.

Telephone Reassurance. For information write for AARP or NRTA Catalog of Publications and Materials, to: AARP National Headquarters, 1909 K Street NW, Washington, D.C. 20049.

Organizations:

National Institute on Adult Day Care (NIAD), 600 Maryland Avenue SW, West Wing 100, Washington, D.C. 20024.

National Voluntary Organizations for Independent Living for the Aging, 600 Maryland Avenue SW, West Wing 100, Washington, D.C. 20024.

Retired Senior Volunteer Program (RSVP), Action, Older Americans Volunteer Programs, 806 Connecticut Avenue NW, Washington, D.C. 20525.

Medical Information and Health Care

Books:

The Dartmouth Institute for Better Health and the Dartmouth Medical School. *Medical and Health Guide for People Over Fifty.* Glenview, Ill.: Scott, Foresman & Co. (AARP), 1986.

Duncan, Theodore G., M.D. *Over 55—A Handbook on Health.* Philadelphia, Pa.: The Franklin Institute Press, 1982.

Kahn, Ada P., M.P.H. *Help Yourself to Health—Arthritis.* Chicago: Contemporary Books, Inc., 1983.

Kahn, Ada P., M.P.H. *Help Yourself to Health—High Blood Pressure,* Chicago: Contemporary Books, Inc., 1983.

Rose, F. Clifford, and Capildeo, Rudy. *Stroke: The Facts.* New York: Oxford University Press, 1981.

Booklets:

Drugs and the Elderly. NIH Publication No. 79-1449, Revised July 1979. U.S. Department of Health and Human Services, Superintendent of Documents, Washington, D.C. 20402.

The Fitness Challenge in the Later Years: An Exercise Program for Older Americans. Publication Number OHD/AOA 73-20802. May be obtained from U.S. Department of Health and Human Services, Administration on Aging, Washington, D.C. 20201.

Health Aspects of Aging. American Medical Association, 535 N. Dearborn Street, Chicago, Ill. 60610.

Using Medicines Wisely. ADM 78-705. U.S. Department of Health and Human Services, Superintendent of Documents, Washington, D.C. 20402.

Organizations:

American Cancer Society, 777 Third Avenue, New York, N.Y. 10017. (212) 371-2900.

American Diabetes Association, Two Park Avenue, New York, N.Y. 10016. (212) 683-7444.

American Foundation for the Blind, Inc., 15 W. 16th Street, New York, N.Y. 10011. (212) 620-2000.

American Health Care Association, 2500 15th Street NW, Washington, D.C. 20005. (202) 833-2050.

American Heart Association, 7320 Greenville Avenue, Dallas, Tex. 75231. (214) 750-5300.

American Lung Association, 1740 Broadway, New York, N.Y. 10019. (212) 245-8000.

American Medical Association, 535 N. Dearborn Street, Chicago, Ill. 60610.

American Occupational Therapy Association, Inc., 1383 Piccard Drive, Suite 301, Rockville, Md. 20850.

American Physical Therapy Association, 1111 N. Fairfax Street, Alexandria, Va. 22314.

American Red Cross, 17th and D Streets NW, Washington, D.C. 20006. (202) 737-8300.

Arthritis Foundation, 1314 Spring Street NW, Atlanta, Ga. 30309. (404) 872-7100.

Citizens for the Treatment of High Blood Pressure, 1101 17th Street NW, Suite 608, Washington, D.C. 20036. (202) 296-4435.

Living Bank, P.O. Box 6725, Houston, Tex. 77005. (713) 528-2971. Information center to "educate the general public to donate organs."

National Association of the Deaf, 814 Thayer Avenue, Silver Spring, Md. 20910. (Also National Association of Hearing and Speech Agencies.)

National Association of Rehabilitation Facilities, P.O. Box 17675, Washington, D.C. 20015. (703) 556-8848.

National Association for the Visually Handicapped, 305 E. 24th Street, New York, N.Y. 10010.

National Center for Health Promotion & Aging, c/o National Council on Aging, 600 Maryland Avenue SW, West Wing 100, Washington, D.C. 20024.

National Mental Health Association, 1021 Prince Street, Arlington, Va. 22314.

More on Nursing Homes

Articles:

"The Challenge of Choosing a Nursing Home." *Business Week,* November 22, 1982, pp. 122–23, 126.

Conway, Joan McGarry. "The Guilt Factory." *Newsweek,* May 22, 1978, p. 5.

Books:

Burger, Sarah, and Erasmo, Martha N. *Living in a Nursing Home. A Complete Guide for Residents, Their Families, and Friends.* New York: Seabury Press, 1976.

Fox, Nancy. *You, Your Parent, and the Nursing Home.* Bend, Oreg.: Geriatric Press, Inc., 1982.

Vladeck, Bruce C. *Unloving Care—The Nursing Home Tragedy.* New York: Basic Books, Inc., 1980.

West, Katherine L. *What Do I Do: How to Care for, Comfort, and Commune With Your Nursing Home Elder.* AMATA Graphics, P.O. Box 12313, Portland, Oreg. 97212.

Booklets:

How Do I Pay for Nursing Home Care?, Reactions to Nursing Home Admission, and *Thinking About a Nursing Home?* American Health Care Association, 1200 Fifteenth Street NW, Washington, D.C. 20005. (202) 833-2050. A consumer's guide for choosing a long-term care facility.

How to Establish a Resident Council. Available through the Federation of Protestant Welfare, Division on Aging, 281 Park Avenue South, New York, NY. 10010.

Lincoln, M. *Choosing a Nursing Home for the Person With Intellectual Loss.* 1980, The Burke Rehabilitation Center, 785 Mamaroneck Avenue, White Plains, N.Y. 10605.

Nursing Home Care. U.S. Department of Health, Education, and Welfare (now known as The Department of Health and Human Services). Booklet number (HCFA) 77-24902, may be ordered from the U.S. Department of Health and Human Services, Medical Services Administration, Washington, D.C. 20201.

Ombudsman for Nursing Homes: Structure and Process. Publication number 78-20293. U.S. Department of Health and Human Services, Administration on Aging, 300 Independence Avenue SW, Washington, D.C. 20201.

"Patient's Bill of Rights," for copy see page 186.

Selecting a Nursing Home, Nursing Home Advisory & Research Council, Inc., 1981. Available from Concerned Relatives of Nursing Home Patients, 3137 Fairmont Boulevard, Cleveland Heights, Ohio 44118. (216) 321-0403.

Organizations:

Concerned Relatives of Nursing Home Patients, P.O. Box 18820, Cleveland Heights, Ohio 44118. (216) 321-0403. The organization provides education, information, support, and involvement, in all areas involving nursing home residents and their care, including social services, insurance, and legislative acts. Concerned Relatives also publishes a newsletter, *Insights.*

Nursing Home Advisory & Research Council, P.O. Box 18820, Cleveland Heights, Ohio 44118.

Nutrition Helps

Books:

MacDonald, Phyllis. *The Golden Age Cookbook.* Garden City, N.Y.: Doubleday & Company, 1961.

Natow, Annette B., and Heslin, JoAnn. *Geriatric Nutrition.* Boston: CBI Publishing Co., 1980.

Rohrer, Virginia and Norman. *How to Eat Right and Feel Great.* Wheaton, Ill.: Tyndale Publishers, 1976.

Weg, Ruth B. *Nutrition and the Later Years.* Los Angeles: University of Southern California Press, 1978.

Booklets:

Food Guide for Older Folks. USDA Home and Garden Bulletin Number 17. U.S. Government Printing Office No. 1011-03321; *Nutrition and Your Health.* Home & Garden Bulletin No. 232; *Food.* Home & Garden Bulletin No. 228. Science and Education Administration. Stock no. 001-000-03881-8; *Healthy People.* The Surgeon General's Report on Health Promotion and Disease Prevention. Public Health Service, U.S. Department of Health, Education, and Welfare. Stock No. 017-001-00416-2. To obtain copies write to: Superintendent of Documents, U.S. Government Printing Office, Washington D.C. 20402.

Mealplanning for the Golden Years. General Mills, Inc., Nutrition Service Department 5, 9200 Wayzata Boulevard, Minneapolis, Minn. 55440.

The Way to a Man's Heart. American Heart Association, 7320 Greenville Avenue, Dallas, Tex. 75231.

Organizations

National Association of Nutrition & Aging Service Programs, P.O. Box 505, Frankfort, Ind. 46041.

Patient's Bill of Rights

Under federal regulations, nursing homes must have written, updated policies covering the rights and responsibilities of patients, and these must be available to patients and to the public, to ensure that each patient in the facility:

1. Is fully informed, as evidenced by the patient's written acknowledgment, prior to, or at the time of admission and during stay, of these rights and of all rules and regulations governing patient conduct and responsibilities;

2. Is fully informed, prior to or at the time of admission and during stay, of services available in the facility, and of related charges in-

cluding any charges for services not covered under Title XVIII or XIX of the Social Security Act, or not covered by the facility's basic per diem rate;

3. Is fully informed, by a physician, of his medical condition unless medically contraindicated (as documented by a physician, in his medical record), and is afforded the opportunity to participate in the planning of his medical treatment and to refuse to participate in experimental research;

4. Is transferred or discharged only for medical reasons, or for his welfare or that of other patients, or for nonpayment for his stay (except as prohibited by Title XVIII of the Social Security Act), and is given reasonable advance notice to ensure orderly transfer or discharge, and such actions are documented in his medical record;

5. Is encouraged and assisted, throughout his period of stay, to exercise his rights as a patient and as a citizen, and to this end may voice grievances and recommend changes in policies and services to facility staff/or to outside representatives of his choice, free from restraint, interference, coercion, discrimination, or reprisal;

6. May manage his personal affairs, or is given at least a quarterly accounting of financial transactions made on his behalf should the facility accept his written delegation of this responsibility to the facility for any period of time in conformance with state law;

7. Is free from physical and mental abuse, and free from chemical and (except in emergencies) physical restraints except as authorized in writing by a physician for a specified and limited period of time, or when necessary to protect the patient from injuring himself or others;

8. Is assured confidential treatment of his personal and medical records, and may approve or refuse their release to any individual outside the facility, except in case of his transfer to another health care institution, or as required by law or third-party payment contract;

9. Is treated with consideration, respect, and full recognition of his dignity and individuality, including privacy in treatment and in care for his personal needs;

10. Is not required to perform services for the facility that are not included for therapeutic purposes in his plan of care;

11. May associate and communciate privately with persons of his choice, and send and receive his personal mail unopened, unless medically contraindicated (as documented by his physician in his medical record);

12. May meet with, and participate in activities of social, religious, and community groups at his discretion, unless medically contraindicated (as documented by a physician in his medical record);

13. May retain and use his personal clothing and possessions as space permits, unless to do so would infringe upon the rights of other patients, and unless medically contraindicated (as documented by his physician in his medical record);

14. If married, is assured privacy for visits by his/her spouse; if both are in-patients in the facility, they are permitted to share a room, unless medically contraindicated (as documented in the medical record by the attending physician).

The Nursing Home Checklist

	Yes	No
1. Does the home have a current state license?	☐	☐
2. Does the administrator have a current state license?	☐	☐
3. Is the home certified to participate in financial assistance programs?	☐	☐
4. Does the home provide special services such as a specific diet or therapy which the patient needs?	☐	☐
5. Location:		
• Pleasing to the patient?	☐	☐
• Convenient for patient's personal doctor?	☐	☐
• Convenient for frequent visitors?	☐	☐
• Near a hospital?	☐	☐
6. Accident prevention:		
• Well-lighted inside?	☐	☐

	Yes	No
• Free of hazards underfoot?	☐	☐
• Chairs sturdy and not easily tipped?	☐	☐
• Warning signs posted around freshly waxed floors?	☐	☐
• Handrails in hallways and grab bars in bathrooms?	☐	☐

7. Fire safety:
   - Meets federal and state codes? ☐ ☐
   - Exits clearly marked and unobstructed? ☐ ☐
   - Written emergency evacuation plan? ☐ ☐
   - Frequent fire drills? ☐ ☐
   - Exit doors not locked on the inside? ☐ ☐
   - Stairways enclosed and doors to stairways kept closed? ☐ ☐

8. Bedrooms:
   - Open into hall? ☐ ☐
   - Window? ☐ ☐
   - No more than four beds to a room? ☐ ☐
   - Easy access to each bed? ☐ ☐
   - Drapery (privacy curtain) for each bed? ☐ ☐
   - Nurse call bell (or light) by each bed? ☐ ☐
   - Fresh drinking water at each bed stand? ☐ ☐
   - At least one comfortable chair for each patient? ☐ ☐
   - Reading lights? ☐ ☐
   - Clothes closet and drawers? ☐ ☐
   - Room for wheelchair to maneuver? ☐ ☐
   - Care in selecting roommates? ☐ ☐

9. Cleanliness:
   - Generally clean, even though it may have a lived-in look? ☐ ☐
   - Free of unpleasant odors? ☐ ☐
   - Incontinent patients given prompt attention? ☐ ☐

10. Lobby:
   - Is the atmosphere welcoming? ☐ ☐
   - If also a lounge, is it being used by residents? ☐ ☐
   - Furniture attractive and comfortable? ☐ ☐
   - Plants and flowers? ☐ ☐
   - Certificates and licenses on display? ☐ ☐

Yes No

11. Hallways:
    - Large enough for two wheelchairs to pass with ease? ☐ ☐
    - Hand-grip railings on the sides? ☐ ☐
12. Dining Room:
    - Attractive and inviting? ☐ ☐
    - Comfortable chairs and tables? ☐ ☐
    - Easy to move around in? ☐ ☐
    - Tables convenient for those in wheelchairs? ☐ ☐
    - Food tasty and attractively served? ☐ ☐
    - Meals match posted menu? ☐ ☐
    - Are those who need help receiving it? ☐ ☐
13. Kitchen:
    - Are food preparation, dishwashing, and garbage areas separated? ☐ ☐
    - Food needing refrigeration not standing on counters? ☐ ☐
    - Kitchen help observes sanitation rules? ☐ ☐
14. Activity rooms:
    - Rooms available for patients' activities? ☐ ☐
    - Equipment (such as games, easels, yarn, kiln) available? ☐ ☐
    - Are patients using equipment? ☐ ☐
15. Special-purpose rooms:
    - Rooms set aside for physical examinations or therapy? ☐ ☐
    - Rooms being used for stated purpose? ☐ ☐
16. Isolation room:
    - At least one (one bed) room and bathroom available for patients with contagious illness? ☐ ☐
17. Toilet facilities:
    - Convenient to bedrooms? ☐ ☐
    - Easy for wheelchair patient to use? ☐ ☐
    - Sink convenient? ☐ ☐
    - Nurse call bell? ☐ ☐
    - Hand grips on or near toilets? ☐ ☐
    - Bathtubs and showers with nonslip surfaces? ☐ ☐

Yes No

18. Grounds:
    - Can residents get fresh air? ☐ ☐
    - Are there ramps to help handicapped? ☐ ☐
19. Medical:
    - Physician available in emergency? ☐ ☐
    - Private physician allowed? ☐ ☐
    - Regular medical attention assured? ☐ ☐
    - Thorough physical immediately before or upon admission? ☐ ☐
    - Medical records and plan of care kept? ☐ ☐
    - Patient involved in developing plans for treatment? ☐ ☐
    - Other medical services (dentists, optometrists, etc.) available regularly? ☐ ☐
    - Freedom to purchase medicines outside home? ☐ ☐
    - Monthly review of medications by physician? ☐ ☐
20. Hospitalization:
    - Arrangement with nearby hospital for transfer when necessary? ☐ ☐
21. Nursing Services:
    - R.N. responsible for nursing staff in a skilled nursing home? ☐ ☐
    - L.P.N. on duty day and night in a skilled nursing home? ☐ ☐
    - Trained nurse's aides and orderlies on duty in homes providing some nursing care? ☐ ☐
22. Rehabilitation:
    - Specialists in various therapies available when needed? ☐ ☐
23. Activities program:
    - *Individual patient preferences observed?* ☐ ☐
    - Group and individual activities? ☐ ☐
    - Residents encouraged but not forced to participate? ☐ ☐
    - Outside trips for those who can go? ☐ ☐
    - Volunteers from the community work with the patients? ☐ ☐
24. Religious observances:
    - Arrangements made for patient to worship as he pleases? ☐ ☐
    - Religious observances a matter of choice? ☐ ☐

Yes   No

25. Social services:
    • Social worker available to help residents and families? ☐ ☐
26. Food:
    • Dietician plans menus for patients on special diets? ☐ ☐
    • Variety from meal to meal? ☐ ☐
    • Meals served at normal mealtimes? ☐ ☐
    • Plenty of time for each meal? ☐ ☐
    • Snacks available? ☐ ☐
    • Food delivered to patients' rooms? ☐ ☐
    • Help with eating given when needed? ☐ ☐
27. Grooming:
    • Barbers and beauticians available? ☐ ☐
28. General atmosphere friendly and supportive? ☐ ☐
29. Residents retain human rights:
    • May participate in planning treatment? ☐ ☐
    • Medical records kept confidential? ☐ ☐
    • Can veto experimental research? ☐ ☐
    • Have freedom and privacy to attend to personal needs? ☐ ☐
    • Married couples may share room? ☐ ☐
    • All have opportunities to socialize? ☐ ☐
    • May manage own finances if capable, or obtain accounting if not? ☐ ☐
    • May decorate own bedrooms? ☐ ☐
    • May communicate with anyone without censorship? ☐ ☐
    • Are not transferred or discharged arbitrarily? ☐ ☐
30. Administrator and staff available to discuss problems? ☐ ☐
    • Patients and relatives can discuss complaints without fear of reprisal? ☐ ☐
    • Staff responds to calls quickly and courteously? ☐ ☐
31. Residents appear alert unless very ill? ☐ ☐
32. Visiting hours accommodate residents and relatives? ☐ ☐
33. Civil rights regulations observed? ☐ ☐
34. Visitors and volunteers pleased with home? ☐ ☐